THE
TRUE MEANING
OF THE LAST SUPPER:
WELCOMING OTHERS

*A MISSIONAL APPROACH TO
HOLY COMMUNION*

DONALD R. STEELBERG

THE
TRUE MEANING
OF THE LAST SUPPER:
WELCOMING OTHERS

A MISSIONAL APPROACH TO HOLY COMMUNION

Then Moses and Aaron, Nadab, and Abihu, and seventy of the elders of Israel went up, and they saw the God of Israel. Under his feet there was something like a pavement of sapphire stone, like the very heaven for clearness. God did not lay his hand on the chief men of the people of Israel; also they beheld God, and they ate and drank.

—Exodus 24:9–11

"…I confer on you, just as my Father has conferred on me, a kingdom, so that you may eat and drink at my table in my kingdom…

—Luke 22:29–30

DONALD R. STEELBERG

WESTBOW
PRESS
A DIVISION OF THOMAS NELSON

WestBow Press books may be ordered through booksellers or by contacting:

WestBow Press
A Division of Thomas Nelson
1663 Liberty Drive
Bloomington, IN 47403
www.westbowpress.com
1-(866) 928-1240

ISBN: 978-1-4497-1601-1 (sc)
ISBN: 978-1-4497-1602-8 (hc)
ISBN: 978-1-4497-1600-4 (e)

Library of Congress Control Number: 2011927349

Printed in the United States of America

WestBow Press rev. date: 8/18//2011

Dedicated to the congregations of
First Mennonite Church, Wadsworth, Ohio,
and
Lorraine Avenue Mennonite Church,
Wichita, Kansas,
who suffered the birth pangs of these thoughts.

CONTENTS

INTRODUCTION

"It's not easy," he repeated. "The English are not a deeply religious people. Even many of those who attend divine service do so from habit. Their acceptance of the sacrament is perfunctory. I have yet to meet the man whose hair rose at the nape of his neck because he was about to taste the blood of his dying Lord."

—Vicar Keach

JL Carr, A Month in the Country

This is an invitation to look at Jesus' Last Supper as it was understood in the era immediately following his death and resurrection. It is a look at what the Last Supper means with regard to understanding Communion today, worship, and what may be a surprising, evangelical welcoming of outsiders. This examination emphatically rejects using the Supper to discipline anyone who does not agree with church teaching, a practice that has happened throughout the centuries and in our recent United States political life.

Strong biblical attestations would appear to justify the understandings most prevalent today. Paul says that Jesus "was handed over to death for our trespasses and was raised for our justification" (Romans 4:25). I hope to show that Paul's understanding can be both accepted and interpreted differently, as can the Last Supper, which began as suppers did around various dining room tables to which neighbors were invited and Jesus' stories were told.

A growing difference in approach to the Supper occurred even in the first century CE, forsaking the understanding Jesus intended. This new understanding became the dominant approach to Holy Communion by the third century. Charted here are the developments in the first century that changed the original understanding; also charted here are the changes the intervening years have brought. I maintain that the earliest understanding is still justifiable, as it was Jesus' original intention for the Supper held in his name.

My tradition is often apologetic for the way it observes Communion. Liturgists say that we do not observe it often enough; or it is an add-on, not integral to our worship. We are uncertain of its meaning. We should be apologetic for failing Jesus' intention for the Supper: it is an icon into the story of his life and teaching, a welcoming, joyful invitation to everyone. We do not need to apologize because the hair at the nape of our necks does not rise at the invitation to commune.

Two thousand years of church history must be learned from and built upon. At each stage, understanding grew out of the need of the day. Understanding this need can provide learning for us. If we want to stop at one of the stages on the way, that is all right, but could first century practice have something special to offer? Granting that the Holy Spirit has led the church into new truth concerning the Supper, the tradition which developed over the years has been blessed. That blessing need not exclude a defense of what I will develop. The Spirit's direction for leading the church into all truth may still be reformed, as it has been.

What I contest here is the contention that a particular era, say, the third and fourth centuries, had an understanding of the Supper that is superior to our understanding of Jesus' intention and the practice at the beginning of the Christian era. It was John Henry Newman who made peace with his move to Rome by observing that what had stopped him was Rome's elaborate worship, the dominant place of the Virgin Mary, and the overweening authority of the pope. However, he changed his mind about Rome when he saw that in the primitive church there had been developing its doctrine; without that development, we would not have the doctrines of the incarnation and the Trinity, also alien to that first century.

Does a developing understanding of Communion lock us into only one approach?

When that judgment is made, it rests on a failure to recognize the screens that filtered and changed the meaning of Jesus' words: "This is my body. This is my blood." These screens are the historical developments of the first century, the Augustinian overlay of the fourth century, and the controversies of the sixteenth century.

My concern is that Communion developed into a ritual, the only appropriate measure of worship in a great part of the church; or, as in my own tradition, Communion developed into a periodic form that worship takes that is usually quite burdened. I do not have trouble with ritual per se, as some in my tradition do, but I do not think that Jesus meant for the Supper to become the ritual of salvation that it came to be. My hope is to show how this developed and how it may be given different meaning.

This is the thesis: believers in Jesus' acts met around tables in homes for fellowship. That is what they understood Jesus had told them to do. They understood that the act of eating together represented the story of Jesus' life and salvation truth. As Jesus had opened his life and life itself to them in the act of eating with others, they could reenact his life with them by sharing meals with others in their homes. Their communion strengthened their faith, and its invitational nature added to their number.

These early believers' understanding of Passover at this time was in keeping with their heritage; it was an invitation to the future and, indeed, a joyful celebration of leaving the past. Its celebratory nature is affirmed by the sense of threat that it presented to the Roman government.

The supper was not worship at first, but it was Holy Communion. As happens when you eat with others, stories were told. In the young church, these stories became the stories repeated in the Gospels. They were later arranged, as history is, from different points of view. In these stories, the understanding of Holy Communion developed. We think of them as having been handed to the church, when, in reality, it was the young church that developed them.

At the core of the New Testament are "eating stories": the welcoming of persons outside the circle—tax collectors, the poor, persons of doubtful reputation, opponents, and so on. Later, Gentiles were welcomed. The accounts of meals in Jesus' ministry and teaching were a startling germ that captured his followers' imaginations. The young church continued these meals, but as tradition developed, the core of welcoming fellowship was lost.

Understanding the development of the Supper in the critical years of 30 to 100 CE shows that what happened to believers, what formed their belief, shaped their understanding of Communion. In their day, gospel writers—Paul and, I will argue, James—shaped the common view of the Supper.

We have the accounts of Jesus' life gathered in Acts, as well as the argument that developed between Paul and Peter, a contentious argument about hypocrisy and the true meaning of kosher. We know of the persecution of believers, but on the pages of the book of Acts, little is made of the effect these events had on understanding Communion. We have to read between the lines.

The book of Acts tells us that the disciples and new believers met in family fellowship in the rich tradition of their past. We can imagine mothers saying the prayers as they lit the candles, children asking questions, fathers giving a blessing, neighbors being invited, stories of faith being shared, and discussion of their and their community's common needs. In this setting, around tables, the community of faith grew.

As the years progressed, the early followers were put out of the synagogues. We would be, too, if we challenged the common belief. No doubt these followers of Christ missed the formal structure of praise and instruction they had known in the synagogue. So, they copied its worship, patterning it early on after the account in Luke's gospel when Jesus attends a service in his home synagogue. After this, they began the first of their borrowings from the culture around them, setting up a pattern like the Roman social clubs, with meals and lectures after the last course of the dinner. John's gospel suggests adoption of this pattern.

Three factors come to influence the young church's understanding of Communion. The first is the persecution the believers would face, which made them draw into themselves and restrict communing to being with those they knew and could trust.

The second is their growing understanding of who Jesus was and, particularly, of the stories of his birth that affected their thinking.

The third, almost nowhere else considered, is the growing influence of James, the brother of Jesus, who led the young church in coming to understand the Supper as a means of keeping the law and understanding it as a replacement for the sacrificial system of the temple—complete with priests.

These three factors changed believers' understanding of the bread and the cup with the passing years. By the end of the century, Communion would no longer be an enacted story at the dining room table, passing on a tradition. Bread and cup would become objects of devotion. The site would move from the home to a gathering of believers, "church," and later, for some, to basilicas. Celebrating parents would be replaced by consecrating priests.

Because of persecution, the welcoming circle closed to admit only believers in good standing. The atmosphere of celebration changed to sorrowful penitence. From daily and then weekly celebration, they would move in later years to yearly and even deathbed observance.

The "why" of these developments, which began toward the end of the first century, has not been examined for the effect it had on the meaning of Holy Communion in today's worship. Was it an embracing, welcoming act, or was it a means to salvation? Was it both?

Holy Communion developed on two tracks.

Track one is the table fellowship of Jesus. Jesus' ministry begins with eating. He saw table fellowship as a sign of God's reign, a sign of fellowship in the world to come. The first miracle that he wrought, as John says, changing the water to wine at the wedding in Cana of

Galilee, is a sign of future promise, but all the common meals are signs. A wedding ring is a sign. So is a meal, according to Jesus.

Three conclusions follow: First, the meal is a sign that God's reign was present in Jesus' teaching. His teaching gets him into trouble with Rome and causes his death. Rome could not afford a challenge to the political hegemony that communitarian meals invited—especially the discussion and expectation of a different kingdom's hegemony—or the division among its Jewish population these meals caused.

Second, the meal had a welcoming nature: Jesus ate with outcasts and sent his disciples on missions free of the shibboleths of not eating with those whose customs differed from their own. Even for Jesus, meals were restricted to the household of faith, because he understood his ministry was to his own people. He knew that the supper would only become a welcoming meal for all people in the revelation that would come to Peter. We often miss the church's development of Jesus' thought and the ways the Spirit has led us into all truth.

Third, for Jesus, the meal was not intended to be a ritual for forgiveness but the embodiment of forgiveness. Zacchaeus was welcomed, and then he repented. Forgiveness found in that welcome results in amending one's life, as his story shows us. Jesus was not intending to control in the way that church hierarchies contend today, but to welcome.

Track two is that Holy Communion becomes a ritual for the forgiveness of sin early in the church's life, probably through the leadership of James, the brother of Jesus. James influenced Mark, and Mark's ideas were further developed by Matthew. In this development, the meal becomes a sacrifice. We have only church history's testimony to this development; there is no paper trail in the New Testament explaining it. As Dom Gregory Dix clearly says of the development over the years: "It is important for the understanding of the whole future history of the liturgy to grasp the fact that Eucharistic worship from the outset was not based on scripture at all, whether of the Old or New Testament, but solely on tradition." (page 3)

The ritual words in Matthew at the supper, "for the forgiveness of sins" (26:28), must be read in a developmental context, as an insertion at a later date, a gloss. It arises because of Matthew's appropriation of James' understanding of the Supper, his approach from Leviticus.

Jesus appears to have understood forgiveness to mean that one would be welcome into the Father's arms without preconditions other than coming to oneself, as the story of the Prodigal tells us. Its development in the New Testament changed this, positing forgiveness in terms of the sacrificial system of Hebrew faith.

This means that we have to understand that the Scripture story does not develop on a straight trajectory as we might suppose from reading straight on from Matthew through Revelation: Jesus' birth, ministry, death, and resurrection; the promise of everlasting life; and the birth of the church affect the way the story is told. The Scripture story develops through the lens that the resurrection later provides. Here is Jaroslav Pelikan, a foremost church historian:

> From the early chapters of the Book of Acts we get a somewhat idealized picture of a Christian community that continued to follow the Scriptures, the worship, and the observances of Jewish religious life. The members of the church at Jerusalem followed James, who, as the "brother of the Lord," was a kind of "caliph," in refusing to acknowledge a fundamental cleavage between their previous life and their new status. Clearly, they recognized that something new had come, not something brand new, but something newly restored and fulfilled. Even after the fall of Jerusalem in AD 70, these "Nazarenes" maintained continuity with Judaism. Especially in the period before A.D. 70, the tensions within Jewish thought were reflected also in the beginnings of Christian theology. The party headed by James manifested significant analogies with Palestinian Judaism, while the missionary party which eventually came to be identified

with Paul, as with Christian apologists of the second century, reflected certain affinities with the Jewish thought of the Hellenistic diaspora. More fundamental than these parallels, however, is the conflict between Hellenistic Jews and Hellenistic Jewish-Christians over the question of the continuity of Christianity with Judaism. (page 13)

The forces coming together, then, in this second track were James's leadership, attested by Paul's records of his visits to James, and the rulings James made at the Jerusalem Council (Acts 15). He was a caliph, or first pope. Some scholars suggest that the gospel record is not fair to James's presence during Jesus' ministry, his name being confused with another. Given the developing tradition, it appears that he disagreed with Jesus' invitation to look at tradition differently. And then persecution and the developing understanding of the incarnation contributed to making bread and wine holy.

This is the thesis, then, of the two-track development. Table fellowship, sharing the good news of Jesus, becomes a ritual for forgiveness of sin mediated by a priest or bishop.

Some may see this examination as a too-secular or non-miraculous view of Communion. I see it as a human view of what Jesus was about. This connects to the ancient human-divine argument about Jesus himself. As he was fully human, so is the Supper. And yet, "human" does not disallow the tradition's deeper, greater dimension. It is the human aspect that needs to be lifted up in all its mystery in these days because of our adulation of the sacrament. The human aspect is also holy.

Consider the story and what a return to the fellowship of the early "Acts" church might mean for us today. It might not only mean a return to family fellowship around tables, but also an awareness of how such family fellowship can instruct and enrich our worship. Jesus' table fellowship welcomes all of the human family.

This book is the result of my journey with the sacrament of Holy

Communion and an ongoing personal and pedagogical dialogue that I have had for forty years in my mind and in my ministry. I cannot cite all those I have learned from, but the debt is clear. I am particularly indebted to Bruce Chilton, whose work on Jesus' meals I found only in the late nineties, solving many riddles for me. I am also indebted to him for directing me to Hans Lietzmann, and to Hans Lietzman for his insights on broadening the invitation to all who commune. I am additionally indebted to Willi Marxsen and Eduard Schweizer. My debt is also to Markus Barth; to John Dominic Crossan's studies of the birth of Christianity; to Ben Witherington III; and to Jon D. Levenson for his study of Jewish thought on atonement in the first century CE. I hope to communicate their scholarship to persons in the pews. I have chosen to write this without footnotes, but I have included a bibliography, recourse to which will bear out what I say here.

I owe a debt of gratitude as well to my friend and seminary classmate, David F. Noble, PhD, for his careful attention to the argument and for grammatical corrections.

Join the dialogue with me.

My Communion Odyssey

I was born into the Sheridan Evangelical Church in Denver, Colorado, where my father was a pastor while he finished his schooling at the University of Colorado and Iliff Theological Seminary. The denomination was in name Evangelical, but it was in all practices Methodist. Early on, or so I was told, Bishop Asbury had not accepted the church into Methodism because its members had refused to drop the German language. By the time I came along, all was English, and soon the Evangelical would become the "E" in the Evangelical United Brethren Church and then the "U" in the United Methodist Church.

My earliest memory of Communion is being left out of it.

Communion was observed at the altar rail; I do not remember how often. I do remember when I was five, going downstairs in the Boulder Church, which was just across the street from the University of Colorado, University Heights Evangelical Church—now sociology offices for the university—where my father had been transferred in the appointment system, and the women were washing the little glass Communion cups. I was allowed to drink the leftover grape juice and eat the leftover little squares of white bread. In my experience, the women of the church were always especially good to their pastor's children. When my father heard of it, he was upset. The bread and grape juice had been consecrated, he said, and it was wrong for my sisters and me to finish it. I would not know until years later that I was entitled, having been baptized. That was my introduction to transubstantiation!

(My odyssey will be continued.)

1: How It All Began

Originally, there were no worship services as we know them in the churches of the Acts. The word *church* entered the story early, but it would be better to speak of the gatherings, or the assembly, of the believers. That is also a more exact translation of *ecclesia*. Both Paul and Luke recorded that Jesus' followers met for table fellowship, the breaking of bread.

Originally, Communion services as we know them did not exist. These people of the Way understood that Jesus had called them to experience his presence as they ate their daily meals. Breaking bread was a synonym for eating. Gradually, recalling Emmaus, it would come to have the double meaning we associate with the term today. It was to these meals that neighbors were invited, and it was through them that their numbers grew as these neighbors were invited to believe.

In truth, perhaps the numbers were not so great. Some idealizing is going on. Winning adherents when you are a persecuted minority is a cause for rejoicing. American Sociologist Rodney Stark has argued for a slow but steady growth and has noted that even the Latter Day Saints in our era have experienced more growth through friendship evangelism than through sending their young missionaries. For those of us who feel guilty that we are not evangelists, the good news is table fellowship.

There were preaching occasions when the apostles explained the faith to great numbers of people in settings that might be similar to what we have come to know as evangelistic campaigns. Peter preached to crowds of people, and a story of the lengthiness of one of Paul's sermons at a Saturday evening carry-in meal tells us a young man fell asleep and tumbled out of a third-story window.

But this was not preaching as we know it; these were more like lectures. And these were not services of worship set in the context of adoration, reflection on a Psalm and a reading, and prayers of confession and intercession. We would more likely find them to be like a Billy Graham rally lately, but without the music. Faith claims were being made, but it was not worship.

At this early time, Christ's followers continued to worship in the Friday evening synagogue services. Then, on the evening of the Sabbath (Saturday), they would gather for supper. Later, they moved this time to Sunday evening in order to distance themselves from their Jewish roots. When Paul arrived in a community, he sought out the Friday service at the synagogue as a matter of course. The synagogue service evidently allowed him an opportunity to make a claim for the new day that had come, which is more than our worship services do today. Imagine having someone stand in one of our services to press the truth claims of a different interpretation, another religion! No wonder the Christians began to be put out of the synagogues.

Some commentators on Matthew's gospel suggest that Matthew was writing as Christians were being put out of the synagogues in Syria. This would explain some of the animus against the Pharisees that you find in his gospel and makes it important that we temper our understanding of the descriptions of them. Our definition of a Pharisee tends to peg them more as hypocrites than as the protectors of the faith that they were. That Jesus disagreed with their interpretation should not permit us to use the descriptor loosely.

Being put out of the synagogues soon became the rule everywhere. It was unnerving. They probably began to doubt their own truth. The complicating fact was that there was so much good to be kept from the old way. After all, it was the synagogue that was instituted to replace the temple in the dark days of the captivity in Babylon. It was the synagogue, gatherings of perhaps as few as ten men reading their Scriptures and praying together, that had kept Judaism alive and vital during the exile after the destruction of the temple and during the rise of the Roman Empire. The synagogue had four hundred years of history. Father and grandfather and great-grandfather had been faithful in their attendance (never mind that mother and grandmother and great-grandmother had to sit in an ante room!). Jesus himself, they recalled, had gone to the synagogue regularly: *as was his custom.* It is in this setting that we must understand the developing argument in the gatherings of how to keep the faith. They had to ask themselves, "What was the meaning of Christ's death? How is our understanding affected by our understandings of Scripture and tradition? How are we different?"

And so, when cast out, they decided not to limit themselves to Sunday evening suppers. They set up Sunday morning worship services in honor of the resurrection on the first day of the week. They copied the synagogue pattern of a hymn followed by a reading from Scripture, followed by a commentary on what had been read, and ending with prayers of praise and intercession. Contrary to synagogue practice, they allowed women to attend. Apparently there was some difference over whether women could speak in the gathering. Paul, writing to the Corinthians, said he did not allow it, which probably suggests it was already happening. Elsewhere, we read of Philip the evangelist's four unmarried daughters who had the gift of prophecy. Whether they spoke in the gatherings is not said, but prophets usually speak out, and they must have been heard somewhere if they were known as prophets. Certainly, Priscilla's formative work would also seem to contradict the rule of silence for women. The testimony is that she took Paul in hand and instructed him; this is rather amazing, and it makes an argument against the silencing of women.

Nothing is said that would indicate that the Supper was observed in connection with these morning services. Church historians tell us that the supper for many years, well into the second century, continued to be reserved for the Sunday evening hour as a meal, later to be called the agape. The supper continued in that evening hour for years even after the Eucharist was added to the morning service.

In this way, they kept the tradition of resurrection day meals that Jesus had shared with his disciples, and the sense of a meal rather than a rite was maintained. Even when the Eucharist was added to the morning service, deacons would separate worshipers, and only believers were allowed to attend.

Paul tells us that Jesus blessed the cup after the Last Supper, suggesting that the Supper was eaten after the blessing of the bread at the beginning of the meal, as had been the Jewish custom, with the cup of blessing at the end—and only one cup. Perhaps by the fifties in Paul's wing of the church, a ritual had developed placing bread and cup together. The ritual was expanded, and the words "of the covenant" from Exodus were added.

This is how Exodus would have resonated:

> Moses took the blood and threw it upon the people, and said, "Behold the blood of the covenant which the Lord has made with you in accordance with all these words." Then Moses and Aaron, Nadab, and Abi'hu, and seventy of the elders of Israel went up, and they saw the God of Israel; and there was under his feet as it were a pavement of sapphire stone, like the very heaven for clearness. And he did not lay his hand upon the chief men of the people of Israel; they beheld God, and ate and drank. (Exodus 24:8–11)

This becomes a vignette most important for communing and joining the Hebrew and Christian Scriptures. The cup of the covenant was being shared among them; they were eating and drinking in this new, heaven-like era! God had picnicked with them after Mount Sinai and Mount Calvary!

Two consequences follow from the Sunday evening agape. As a Sunday observance, the agape's theme was a joyful resurrection. It would not have the solemnity of the Passover/passion for some years to come. It was a people's supper, a carry-in like what we know today, with the purpose of celebrating and also inviting friends into an evangelical purpose. This tradition carried into the second century when the non-catechized or unbelieving friends and neighbors would not have been allowed to participate in the morning Eucharist.

The liturgy in the second century—the *Didache,* or *The Teaching of the Twelve Apostles*—shows that the Christians met at agape services to celebrate the breaking of the bread. The church's beliefs were recited, and in their prayers, they asked for the heavenly parousia to come as Revelation 22:20 would promise, while proclaiming at the same time that parousia had begun for them. The service was not a memorial for the death of Jesus or for his body and the blood of the covenant; nor was it a remembrance of the Last Supper on the night of his betrayal. The thanksgiving for the cup was for the holy vine of David, revealed through Jesus; the thanksgiving for the bread was for the life and knowledge given through Jesus. Here was a supper with no reference to the tradition that had developed in Mark and Paul.

In our day of instant communication, we may forget how isolated and distant each developing tradition could be, how each was authentic though different. We homogenize the accounts and so fail to see a multiplicity of beginnings that should be equally honored as original.

Evidently, then, in the first hundred years, two traditions developed: an agape tradition celebrating the welcoming meals of Jesus, their promise of journey to the heavenly banquet; and a sacrifice tradition of remembrance of Jesus' death. This is seen most clearly in Matthew and thus is assumed in the other accounts.

It may be that the shift in emphasis in the Passover theme, heavy with betrayal and self-examination, was a pastoral decision on Paul's part to moderate the unruliness of the Corinthian carry-in dinners. If you have a cultural milieu that allows celebration to be rowdy, even drunken, what do you do to rein it in? Shift its purpose from the freedom of the resurrection to the self-examination of the supper. *Is it I, Lord, who have betrayed you?* The problem is that once you have made this shift, it is difficult to return to the free-flowing joy of the resurrection, as church history has shown us. Paul concentrated on the breaking of the covenant found in meals and the breaking of fellowship, not on the forgiveness of sin.

Other influences than a rowdy Corinthian church would shape these traditions. For one, early believers patterned their meetings after current social custom.

The intriguing hint of the discourse after the supper in the upper room in John's gospel is that this was likely a custom borrowed from *Roman* neighbors. Roman social clubs had a meal, and after the wives and children had departed, the men enjoyed some drinking, perhaps some entertainment, such as dancing women or a lecture by a popular philosopher. Why not adapt this to the Sunday evening agape meal? And, so, perhaps they did. John's gospel is presented in this form, perhaps reflecting supper practices at the time: discourse was followed by action, story, and commentary. He presents a long discourse after Judas leaves the Last Supper that continues until the account picks up again with Jesus and the disciples moving to the garden. The discourse prepares the disciples for how they are to live and that the resource for their life is the true vine.

Another pattern would have been caused by the developing hostility these early believers found themselves in. With persecution, they had to screen attendance. Misconstruing their message, enemies reported the new Christians unfairly to the authorities. Their allegiance to the Lord was an affront to the empire; they were cannibalistic: *eat my body; drink my blood.* As the years passed, the meal and worship were combined, and only the faithful were invited to the meal. A welcoming meal became a closed meal through no real fault of their own.

Something else happened in persecution: it became necessary to hold meetings in secret. At first, the secrecy did not greatly affect the meaning of what they were doing. These followers were reenacting the life that Jesus had called them to, sharing peace over a simple meal of bread and wine. They began to meet early in the morning before going off to work, preparing themselves for the events of the day in the solidarity of friends facing the same world. Praying, giving thanks, receiving encouragement, remembering the words and life of Jesus, and pledging themselves to live like him helped them face the day.

In the hurried moments of the early morning in these years of persecution, they gathered to repeat to one another the words of Jesus, "This is my body; this is my blood." This reminded them of the way they were to live that day, strengthening them for the task of living like Jesus throughout all of the day's encounters, encouraging them to risk even as Jesus had risked his life for them. These are actions, verbs. Celebrating was lifting up the action the Supper called them to rather than an appraisal of the elements themselves.

Some of their fellow believers could not risk coming out to these early morning or late night meetings; there were widows and poor members needing help. So, the thought came: "Why not take some of the bread and wine we have shared here to encourage them in our solidarity?" And so they did.

Was it in this simple act of solidarity that something else happened? Did the elements of bread and wine become holy because of the risk taken? Perhaps the story of David's refusal to drink the water purchased by his warriors' at Bethlehem struck a chord with them. Because of their sacrifice while his own life was in peril, he considered the water too holy to assuage his thirst and poured it onto the ground.

Did bread and wine in these terrible times take on the very nature of the body and blood of Jesus they were to represent? Was it the death of Jesus, Lamb of God, which turned their thoughts to the sacrificial system of old? John the Baptist salutes Jesus as the Lamb of God on their first meeting. A tie with sacrifice is strong. We will see that this was true also of popular Jewish theology of the day.

Or was it that under the dread forms of persecution, a sense of guilt arose for which the supper became absolution? We know how that happens, the interior dialogue we hold with ourselves when something has gone wrong. *Is it something I have done? Have I, we, lived in such a way, failing to trust, to share the good news, that God would send this trouble on us to make us change our ways?* Did this add a new layer of meaning to the elements?

Something happened to change the emphasis from the action to the content. Perhaps it was a sense of guilt over their circumstances. Perhaps it was a disagreement over the meaning Jesus had intended by using a supper to symbolize his good news.

7

The division occurred very early. The book of Acts remembers forty years later that Peter had to wrestle with his understanding of how far-reaching the kosher issues were that Jesus had confronted, and how they were to affect his life and ministry. Called by the Spirit to minister to Cornelius, Peter stayed with him several days. Staying meant eating with Cornelius. So important is this story that its graphic dream is told twice in the space of a few pages. Luke obviously saw it as paradigmatic. The Spirit focused Peter's mind on Jesus' words, clean and unclean. Peter would struggle with this a long time and waffle, as his argument with Paul later shows. Peter was undoubtedly under attack by an element among the new believers who wanted to hold on to the old ways.

Two schools of thought developed, and the argument came to a head in the Council at Jerusalem. Paul had been opening a window of the gospel to the Gentiles, even saying that he was called to them and Peter to the Jews. Paul understood this opening to be freedom from the law and openness to the future.

Some background is missing, but James, the brother of Jesus, apparently became the leader of those followers of Christ wishing to keep the Judaic laws. Paul consulted with James early on, but there is almost no narrative about him, as there is for Peter and Paul—until the Council. Evidently, James was supported by a group of the Pharisees who had come to believe and wanted the laws of Moses strictly kept. At the Council, Peter upstaged Paul by saying that he was first to bring the gospel to the Gentiles. But it was Paul's testimony of the work of the Spirit in the lives of the new Gentile believers that won the day. James then asserted his authority and made a ruling about what the Gentiles must believe, do, and not do. Acts 15 would almost suggest that James, rather than Peter, was the first pope or caliph, as Pelikan put it.

It would be natural for the young followers of Christ to puzzle over what role the first covenant's rules were to play in their lives; it would also be natural for a sense of loss to develop over the sacrificial system and the priestly leadership they had known. The same adjustment had occurred in the exile among the Jews after the loss of the temple, which was when they started writing the Hebrew Torah. The parallel between this and the New Testament writings beginning after the loss of Jesus, these early believers' "temple," is interesting.

It appears that James and his followers wanted to find new ways to keep the Levitical traditions and that this led to a priestly class surfacing early. The deeper issue was whether the new *replaced* the old, an argument that would bear tragic fruit as the church came to see itself as the successor, the replacement, to Judaism. What had Jesus meant in "replacing the law?" It is a question that still resonates today.

A priestly class developed. The second century CE began, and now only a priest could bless the bread and cup. By the thirteenth year of the second century, only a bishop was allowed to consecrate the elements. Things had changed and would continue to change. It naturally developed that these early believers felt it would be best to be like their surrounding culture in order to gain others' tolerance. It would be best to occupy the civil government's available basilicas, adapt their worship to the form of the liturgy of the synagogue, and expect that church leaders, priests, and bishops would comport themselves like the leaders of the city-states.

Leaders often followed rather than led, and protecting the institution and the old ways became paramount. When the Goths invaded, wearing trousers, early believers felt their leadership should keep themselves in robes to preserve the old ways. Instead of admitting the underlying agenda of institutional survival, they gave each piece of clothing an ecclesiastical name in hopes of maintaining it and adding gravitas. In a time of chaos, dramatic portrayal is of utmost importance, and so the surplices over the robes and the ringing of the bell at the consecration would keep the tradition alive for another day.

A funny thing had happened on the way out of the synagogue. Finding a way to replace the structure their religious practice had given their lives, these followers began a process that would make them more like themselves before Jesus came than the table host and guests he had envisioned. While he had come, welcoming sinner and righteous alike, now their table fellowship was closed to those who were "sinful."

While bread and fish and wine had symbolized a foretaste of the heavenly banquet, the elements now became the followers' meager supper. While the supper had once meant the inclusion of mother and father, children and neighbor, and even Judas had not been excluded, now the table was fenced and increasingly inaccessible.

How had it happened? To that question we now turn.

My Odyssey

After that basement "Communion," I did not commune again until I was confirmed in the Swedish Evangelical Free Church where my father had become a professor in Greek New Testament and church history at the Chicago seminary of his birth denomination. The denomination was composed of Swedes who, upon coming to America in the late nineteenth century, had rejected their state's Lutheran Church roots for a Baptist polity ("Swedish" was dropped in 1951). Our church was Lakeview on Sheffield Avenue, one block from Wrigley Field.

I do not remember how often Communion was observed, but following a worship service, communicants kept it and would move into alternate rows so that the pastor and deacons could move down the empty rows to serve us, repeating a Bible verse as we communed. The service was somber, and the pastor was always in a black swallow-tailed coat, striped gray trousers, and a wing-collar shirt and tie. My father had such clothes for the Sundays he occasionally preached. Years later, after I was married, I asked my mother if I could borrow them as a Halloween costume. "No," she said, "they were holy."

Two things come to mind: I remember peeking to see if anyone around me was not communing and thus "in sin." And rather puzzling to me was a brass plate naming the wealthy donor of the Communion table right below the carved words, "This Do in Remembrance of Me."

2: WHAT ELSE HAPPENED?

How did it happen that the simple sharing of a meal symbolizing the way Jesus lived changed to a reenactment of his death? To understand, revisit the biblical story with its history. Circumstances, as we saw in chapter one, affected the young followers' understanding. Was belief enough? Was belief changed by the direction their leaders took?

Two themes galvanize the young church: understanding purity and sacrifice for the forgiveness of sins. A third theme will be examined in the next chapter: who was Jesus?

Read between the lines in the book of the Acts. It seems a straightforward story, but Luke doesn't tell all he knows. He simply shares and witnesses what the disciples were engaged in following the resurrection and ascension and the opposition the witness created with the religious authorities. He reports their sharing of their possessions. He admits there were also disputes among the faithful; not everyone wanted to share, and the Greek believers began to feel their widows were being slighted. Wonderful, human storytelling! These things tested the community. We feel in touch with the humanness of their new situation and that their secrets are not held back. But there is more. Listen to what is said and not said.

Luke tells the story of Peter ministering to the Roman centurion Cornelius and his family. He tells it after Saul enters the community of faith. Chronologically, that may be quite correct, but we begin to see the glimmerings of a contest for community leadership without it being named as such, and the issue of their divergent messages. One question that came up was, what will accepting Paul and Gentile others mean and demand? We know this dynamic and how it affects the way we tell a story.

Luke tells Peter's story twice to underline its significance. The story is full of drama. Peter will later claim that he was the first to preach to the Gentiles. He was. But Paul will say that that ministry was given to him; that while Peter did reach out to the Gentiles, he hypocritically drew back, forfeiting when it came to establishing the Gentiles' new birthrights within the community. Back and forth.

Not explicit in this dialogue is that there is another figure in the wings vying for authority: Jesus' brother James. We have not heard much of this brother in the Gospels. Some scholars claim that we have confused identities when we list the disciples. It is interesting that Jesus entrusts his mother to John when he dies. This broadening of the family of faith ties may have been a slight that James would have felt.

In his letter to the Galatians, Paul mentions consulting Peter and James early on, but we hear sparingly of James in Luke's account. He is present in the upper room after the ascension and again when Peter is released from prison and says, "Tell James." Is he indicating that James has become the head of the believers? I think that most Christians have little idea of James's place in the drama, little understanding of James and his influence.

Luke tells us about the Council at Jerusalem, convened to settle a theological dispute three-fourths of his telling later. It is James who will issue the Council's decision, diplomatically citing Peter as the first one to relate how God had looked favorably upon the Gentiles, but not going as far as the party of the Pharisees in maintaining a requirement of circumcision.

James tells the Gentiles to abstain from the pollution of idols, fornication, things strangled, and from blood. This echoes Leviticus. The decision will be repeated once more to the Gentiles directly, but then it will not be heard of again as a formal requirement for believing. James does not mention Paul in his speech, but Paul has gotten what he wanted and will be sent off on a mission to the wider community.

So we may eat steak tartare except perhaps for health reasons today, but rather than a legal list of requirements, the Holy Spirit will let us judge the requirements of belief. Paul and Silas will shortly tell the Philippian jailer that what (all?) he must do to be saved is to believe in the Lord Jesus. We are not told but would assume that Paul and Silas have had occasion to tell Jesus' story to the jailer.

The deeper question is, has Paul, defining what it means to be a Christian, won the skirmish but not the war?

It is my contention that the understanding of Communion that develops in the church will be closer to James's understanding of salvation than to Paul's initial reporting of the Gentile's inclusion being anointed by the Spirit; that James will lead the young church to an understanding of the Supper as a sacrificial representation of Jesus' death; and that Paul and Mark will follow him in this understanding against the invitation to heavenly fellowship that Jesus offered in his meals.

Where was James coming from? While Jesus was setting people free from the jots and tittles of the law, James valued keeping traditions. Had the situation changed? Building a group's understanding of itself may depend more on hewing to tradition than to the radical change of focusing on the new.

Understanding what happened lies in an appreciation in the young church for the book of Leviticus. This may seem far afield to us, but not for the first century Christians. Leviticus was a book important to their self-understanding as heirs of the Old Testament story, despite the letter to the Hebrews' dismissive citing of its daily sacrifice.

Two themes in a Levitical self-understanding are purity and the need for sacrifice.

Purity

According to the young followers' heritage, their understanding of the faith meant that God's call to them was to be pure, holy, and one. We understand purity in terms of morality and cleanliness, but for the Jew purity was a call to be one as God is one, which had wide implications. Fabrics were not to be mixed; different crops were not to be planted in a field. As Jesus would put it, their eye was to be single. As James would say, believers were not to be double-minded.

Any teaching of a triune God would have shocked these believers. God is one, and Jesus and God's Holy Spirit were a part of this oneness. It took a long time for an idea like the Trinity to gain acceptance in Christian theology, and it took two hundred years for it to become doctrine. The New Testament does not lay out the three in one as the creeds do.

In retelling the story of the Jewish nation, Leviticus tells us that a holy God had given the people of Israel the land of Canaan and that it would be theirs so long as they, too, were holy, pure, and one. Their purity was to be marked by the following of a holiness code, or laws of purity. Foremost in that obedience was the injunction to eat only what was clean. Cleanliness was not a lack of "dirt" as we might define it but what could be understood as being one or whole; not marked by a "cloven" foot. God was holy, one, and so the logic of cleanliness also demanded that the people of God apply this oneness to their lives. Thus, one would eat only of certain categories of creation, not hybrids. This conquest of the Canaanites' land was to be justified by taking up Yahweh's holiness, an understanding that may make us uncomfortable today. It smacks of ethnic cleansing.

Not just the people, but oneself must also be holy or whole or one; and thus, in a practical way, oneself must not stained by any fluids of emission—perhaps understood as a loss of self in that day—when coming to God in worship. One's life, then, was to be marked by a unitary vision across all its engagements, a resonance they may have heard in Jesus' word that the eye be single.

We may have difficulty understanding this concept of holiness cast in terms of oneness. Holiness to us means cleanliness in sanitary or moral terms rather than simplicity. But we may be able to appreciate a concept of the One controlling our outlook. Historically, we find attempts to simplify life in the reforming traditions of hermits, monastic groups, and mystics. The Anabaptists coveted the simple life, raising it to one of five or so tenets they held dear. In our day, we find ourselves on the one hand confused with multiple demands upon our time and our loyalties, longing for a simpler life and seeing things simply, while on the other hand defending a postmodern pluralism with its call to honor the many.

The logic and the promise for Israel was this: if Israel kept this unity, this purity, this understanding of the oneness of God, the land would be Israel's and would remain Israel's. Theoretical meets practical. The land had been given to Israel because the people who were there previously had not kept these purities. Israel felt no need to apologize for this usurpation, as it, too, could lose the land upon failing to be pure. A tenet of faith became: cut off whatever is impure or unclean, violently separating yourself from Gentiles and your own people if they fail in this regard. Holiness was a double-edged sword that both defined oneself and cut off the unclean.

The fear here is deep and broad. During the time of exile in Babylon, the people of Israel had recast their history, writing down its long oral tradition as an explanation for their plight. This fear was to shape the people of Israel's understanding of themselves and their God. Long after it was possible to be ritually pure by making slaughter for sacrifice, long after the loss of the Holy of Holies or having the authority to carry out the death penalties prescribed, the question remained: how could they be pure? The loss of their native land had marked them, and understanding the reasons for their loss resonated, even though the Levitical instructions could not literally apply. What did it still mean to be pure and holy? You can imagine the arguments among them as they tried to be faithful. Their prophets called them to a new understanding about pure hearts rather than keeping tabs.

And then the young followers of the Way became a "new" Israel living in a century that would later be called the first century by a "Christian" faith. They were in the same straits as their ancestors, not ruled by Babylon but Rome. Had they again lost their patrimony because they had not kept the rules of purity? Was being pure keeping kosher and associating and eating only with those who kept the same rules of purity that they did? Not to keep these rules was to be labeled a sinner

Sacrifice

This, in its turn, led these Christians to the second theme of a Levitical faith: sacrifice was needed by a sinner to approach a holy God. Leviticus was detailed in its requirements. In their first century situation, how were they to fulfill these requirements? Once again, the temple had been destroyed. They could no longer spatter the blood of an animal against an altar or send a goat out into the wilderness. They would need to fashion their approach to God in much the same way their ancestors had when the first temple was destroyed; they would return to the prayers and the study of the synagogue.

As they studied Leviticus, they found that sacrifice was not for intentional sin. Sacrifice was intended only for unintentional sins, those actions where by default they had not met God's standard of oneness through ignorance or error or a change in their bodily functions. You approached the altar only after cleansing and fulfilling a waiting period: a day's waiting and washing after a night emission; forty days for a woman after the birth of a male child; and eighty days for a woman after a female birth. There were times and seasons of approach. (Sometimes, keeping a weekly schedule, I long for this approach.)

There was no atonement for an intentional sin. For an intentional sin, you were to be put to death, stoned, or banished. How were they to understand all of this in light of Jesus' coming? He countered the stoning of a woman caught in sin.

As late as the book of Ezekiel, only unintentional sins are atoned for in a sacrificial system (45:20). Intentional sins would find forgiveness in one's prayers (Psalm 51). But by the time of Jesus' ministry, the distinction between the unintentional and the intentional sin had blurred. The definition of sin, missing the mark, could certainly cover the unintentional, a sense of not being right with God or with others (how to handle a fantasy with a female or male friend). In the accounts of Jesus' relationships, he eats with sinners, and he doesn't keep the purity laws (he lets women touch him, for example). The implication is that the people should worry less about unintentional sins than grossly breaking the commandments. As we will see in the next chapter, the distinction between sins, unintentional and intentional, was changing in popular Jewish thought.

The stories of two women are a case in point. The woman with the menstrual flow touched Jesus, making him ritually unclean and unable to go to temple. He healed her. In the common mind, that would also be an act of forgiveness, a deep putting right of something that had gone wrong for her, her oneness taken from her. The woman taken in adultery was dragged before Jesus, the understanding being that there was no forgiveness, no effective sacrifice for her; death by stoning was the law. Jesus forgave her–and, one may say, her accusers. "Neither do I condemn you" astounded her accusers, who left silently. Perhaps they understood that they, too, were forgiven.

So the young believers had to rethink the understanding of sacrifice because of his coming. Their situation now was not that different from that during his ministry. How had he dealt with the questions they were dealing with?

If the distinction now between unintentional and intentional sins was not to be drawn to too fine a point, was Jesus, the Lamb of God, the sacrifice for all sin? If his blood covered all sins, how were they to appropriate that forgiveness? If his blood covered all sin, the argument could become a libertinism: all is forgiven, all is permitted. The apostle Paul would have to confront this argument. Was forgiveness given because of their making their lives pure like his, was it in that meal he had with them before he died, or was it in his death on the cross?

The bottom line in their religious ethos was that purity, oneness, defined Israel. Fail that, and you failed Israel; no harmony was possible. Purity ensured communication with God. Purity determined the survival of the people. The temptation to give into accommodation with Rome was utterly discordant with purity. Yet syncretism was as tempting as it had been in Babylon before their time, and various parties differed on how strictly the rules had to be kept.

There were Sadducees and Pharisees and zealots. Though absent from the story, the Essenes played a part. Our information about these groups' agendas is sketchy. We are told that the Sadducees did not believe in the resurrection of the dead (which should alert us to what importance this belief had developed), but we are not told much else. They appear to have made an accommodation with Rome, finding its hegemony less oppressive and the call to purity less pressing in this political instance than did the Pharisees. It was the Pharisees who had kept the faith through the synagogues during the Exile and after the return.

Issues of conflict that came up at a later date, when the writers of the Gospels were recording their stories, distort what we know of these groups. But it is certain that the focus of their agendas was the question of what it meant to be pure. We see this in repeated instances of conflict with Jesus over the application of the law, particularly with regard to eating customs and washing. We do not know to what party John the Baptist attached himself—perhaps the Essenes. But his preaching is clear: Israel is to purify itself. His doubts about Jesus seem to focus on the fact that Jesus was not on the same page in the keeping of the law. They were not one.

The fact is that Jesus programmatically confronted the issue of purity as the focus of his ministry from the beginning. In an upsetting way, he associated with those who did not or could not keep the law because of economic circumstances. Among those were the revenue contractors and the people of the land, tradespeople and farmers, who were in constant contact with all kinds of people and all kinds of produce; these were common laborers and professionals who could not keep all of the prescriptions for ritual cleanliness. He ate with them. He made up his inner circle of disciples from various strains of Jewish life—fishermen, a tax collector, and apparently a couple of zealots—rather than from one group. When he sent the disciples out on a mission, he told them to eat whatever was set before them—in other words, not to be bound by the kosher laws. We sense that women are an important part of his circle; women in his entourage actually fund him. He is not offended by being touched by women, even by a woman who has a troubling menstrual discharge or another who has a bad reputation.

Jesus walked through Samaria. We are told that he had to go through Samaria, which would have been quite a boundary crossing for his day. But in a more critical way, Jesus crosses and re-crosses the boundaries of a stratified society. His community was a hierarchy based on how faithfully one kept the law. Challenging this, one of his clearest teachings is that purity is not a matter of externals; it is not what goes into a person but what comes out that matters.

His most famous story commends a Samaritan. It is his best story. By definition impure to a faithful Jew, the Samaritan touches a Jew who has been attacked, while pure Jews pass by. The Samaritan picks up the man, nurses his wounds, carries him to an inn, and pays for his care. But we must understand that priest and Levite were not evil; that is the connotation of a history of separation. They were captive to their religious worldview; they were carrying out the command to be faithful as they understood it. We have our own legalities today.

Jesus not only modeled a contrary acceptance, but also he made it part of his good news ministry. And so when he sent out the disciples to evangelize, he told them specifically to stay with whomever invited them in and to eat whatever was set before them. They were not to change hosts at whim or eat their own supply of pita bread and hummus. Can you imagine that?

To understand this, we need to remember that the rules of keeping kosher in his day meant that you could eat only with those who kept the same kosher standards you did. If others did not eat shrimp, you did not. Kosher rules said you ate only with those of like understanding about what is pure, so this direction from Jesus must have upset the disciples' religious outlook. They were being charged with living a new way. They were to be a parable, showing a new day had dawned.

In truth, his new followers were electrified by this freeing approach to association. In a closed and rule-bound society, it was an invitation to live free. But Jesus not only associated across boundaries; he entered into life so gustily that he could be named a glutton and wine-bibber by his detractors; he was quite different from the ascetic John the Baptist. Jesus defended his actions by taking issue with the current understanding of the law. He invited a deeper reading. In the Sermon on the Mount, he specifically reminded his listeners to examine what the bent of their hearts was rather than what was on their hands.

The issue of purity is still with us, as it was for the Pharisees. How could Jesus dine with Jews who were Rome's revenue contractors? These Jews, said the Pharisees, were sinners. We may acknowledge our complicity as sin, but we are probably more half-hearted in our confession than they were in their condemnations. This issue of purity divides the religious community across our communions. For some, baptism has no strictures against supporting war; for others, baptism must mean resisting paying the taxes that fund war.

It is almost impossible to have clean hands today. The Boeing Company builds my community while being built by defense contracts for wars I do not support.

Jesus didn't approach the issue of purity in this way. Purity for him was joyfully seeking to be one with God and God's purposes, and God's purpose was the love of all humankind. It was more important to him to be open and accepting of sinner and Pharisee alike. He went to dinner at Simon the Pharisee's and was offended when Simon didn't hospitably see to the washing of his feet. That was the way he modeled God's love. And it was this openness and acceptance that made him so inviting a teacher to follow. It was this openness that would get him killed.

How ironic and tragic, then, that his welcoming custom of eating with others, children and outsiders alike, should in a short century become a closed ritual of making oneself right with God. His openness, which got him killed, was too threatening to the struggling young church. His meals were not meant to be a sacrifice for atoning sin and failure, but a welcoming sign of God's love. His detractors found it too much to bear in his lifetime. His followers would find it too much to bear after his death.

Israel's history has parallels to the young church's. As the people of Israel had struggled to understand the reasons for their exile, they fastened upon the idea that the exile was retribution for failing to keep the covenant of purity; they had been cast out like those before them. So the members of the young church during its time of exile also argued about failure and chose the purity of the cleanliness covenant. Instead of being open to Jesus' love and the new covenant he had proposed to them at the Last Supper, the church began to close its doors to the outsider who did not keep kosher quite as the church did. The church did this under threat of persecution and death. These early believers' Jewish families and the Roman government alike were threat to them. Pharisees who were joining them were calling for a return to the old ways. It was this conflict that would grow into the full programmatic approach to worship as the young church moved into the second century.

But first, a third theme: who was Jesus?

Odyssey

It may be hard to understand the controversy over purity. But if you grew up, as I did, in an evangelical milieu that was heavy with "don'ts," you may appreciate the quandary Jesus occasioned.

For us, the Sermon on the Mount became a new and oppressive law. Who of us had not lusted in his heart? Jimmy Carter's *Playboy* interview wasn't news to us! The way lust was approached in my youth made you think that you should be able to live without it. Nor were we to go to movies, smoke, drink, or associate with those who did these things. Our separation from the world was a sign of our purity, and if we were faithful, we would be rewarded later. If we failed, we would be excluded from the kingdom. "You would not want to be in a movie, would you, if Jesus returned?" was a statement I heard many times from many different pastors, Sunday school teachers, and even my parents.

I remember how freeing it was when I met believers in InterVarsity Christian Fellowship at Northwestern University who did all these things! It was freeing, yet puzzling, because they had a more vibrant testimony than I had. They could smoke and praise Jesus in the same breath. I realize today that that may be a puzzling non sequitur for most of my readers, but it was this way in my world. Is our fencing the table our own understanding of purity?

3: WHO WAS JESUS?

Something else was beginning to affect the young church's understanding of itself. To that we now turn.

Two strong threads were being woven into the believers' lives in the first century: as they told the story around their dining room tables, they asked who Jesus was and how his death on the cross had saved them. How did his story fit into their Hebrew Scriptures? How did their understanding of tradition affect their understanding of him and their worship?

The first question we turn to in this chapter is, "Who was Jesus?" The question of how the cross saved them will come next.

Jesus came among them, as Mark would later write, as the son of Mary and "perhaps" Joseph (the text at Mark 6:3 is disputed); there were doubts even then about his lineage. His miracles, but primarily his resurrection, led to an early reverencing of his life. The danger would be the exchanging of his humanness for an apparent divinity. At what point did the early believers learn of the birth stories? Because we have Matthew's and Luke's prologues, we forget that the earliest reports of the story by Mark and Paul, and the later report by John, do not claim that Jesus was divine from infancy; nor do they make use of the manger theme as they develop the story of Jesus' life.

In the earliest declaration of Jesus being the Son of God (CE 60?), the apostle Paul says it is because Jesus was resurrected. Paul has no story of a miraculous birth; he tells us only that Jesus was born of a woman. Jesus was human. If Paul knew the birth stories, the theory being that he was part of Luke's crowd, it is all the more interesting that he does not cite the stories as he begins his letter to the Christians in Rome. What did they believe? Paul knew Luke, so why didn't he mention the birth stories?

A steady hagiography developed. Some of this took the form of what would later be labeled Apocrypha. Stories arose of Jesus as a young child magically extending boards he had cut too short in his father's carpenter shop or breathing life into a clay bird he had made or a dead bird he had found. I heard these stories in Sunday school. Not far afield would be suggestions that in his life here he never really touched the ground, but angelically floated four inches above it. We may discount these stories, but they reveal some later perceptions that led believers to appeal to Jesus for magical solutions.

Remembering that Jesus had a temper or could speak poorly of a Syrophoenician woman, calling her a dog, has called forth pious justifications that may not be plain to the reader but attempt to defend a Jesus who would be diminished if allowed to be associated with these "failures." Did he need to learn or have his worldview widened like the rest of us—was he human like us? To this day, there are interpreters who feel they must make excuses for Jesus with regard to this encounter, but a fair understanding of Jesus' humanity is that this woman enabled Jesus to grow spiritually. In his previous encounters before this story, Jesus had been intellectualizing the surpassing of boundaries; in this case he had to experience it to grow.

While the pieties and apocryphal stories can be put aside, a more prominent thread is the story of the birth in Bethlehem. The long Greek and Hebrew tradition of spectacular births has made some wonder about the story's origin: Isaac and Samuel, for example, or Isaiah's promise to Ahaz of a child, Immanuel. We make the Old Testament mythic and the New, historic.

Because of the beauty of the story of Jesus' birth and its dramatic completion of biblical themes, its elemental association with all our Christmas celebrations and longings, it is difficult to see it as literary invention or a completion of literary themes. We are selective in our reading of the "prophecies": he was wounded for our transgressions, but our Sunday school pictures deny he "had no form nor comeliness."

Is that disqualifying? How far are we willing to go in allowing the gospel writers literary invention under the Spirit's direction? Was Jesus John's cousin? It is puzzling that at one point John seems not to know who Jesus is. Is that: "I don't know where you're coming from, I don't agree with you," or is it ignorance of the relationship?

Did a sect that followed John the Baptist tell the birth story to Luke, having heard it from John's mother? The storyline doesn't openly tell us of the sects of the first century story. But there are hints, the chief of which is the seeming need to put down or distance John the Baptist's followers from Jesus' followers, lest John take precedence (thus the interjection, "I am not worthy to tie his shoelace.").

The prologues seem to be a convention for setting the story. The gospel story is Jesus' humanity; the prologues' original intention celebrates this with angels and alleluias. We must be careful not to let the celebration of the birth narratives influence our understanding of salvation and the meaning of eating his body and blood.

Some cannot accept a literal virgin birth. Some do. I do not let it break my fellowship with them. In the same way that I came to accept the historical criticism of the Genesis account, I see how a parallel story of Jesus' new creation might not be held literally. I do not think less of Jesus thereby. I own him as Lord and Savior according to his resurrection; a resurrection that was not just God's stamp of approval on the life he lived and called us to follow, but a resurrection that makes a new creation.

This departs from our received understanding of Scripture's inspiration. But God allowed different interpretations to circulate, such as Paul's "resurrection confirmation," before everything came together in a whole cloth. I marvel at the story of creation and yet also accept the theory of evolution; and so, especially at Christmas time, I marvel at the story of the birth of Jesus and the amazing way it introduces the life of Jesus and presents him as part of Israel's longer story. Hear Mary's Magnificat and you are at once with Israel's prophets, the landless of Jesus' day, and our own world of indentured servants in the world economy.

For an understanding of the tack I am taking in my interpretation, it may be helpful to take a brief detour into the subject of Scripture's inspiration, as it affects my approach to the New Testament's development of the Last Supper.

Inspiration means "God breathed." How Scripture was inspired has never fully been agreed upon—some maintain that there are no errors, practically equating it with dictation, while others allow that there could be errors in transcription. All grant inspiration a strong role in understanding the material.

A long historical debate regarding the inspiration of the Hebrew Scriptures began with the belief that Moses wrote the Pentateuch. Some people then challenged the belief, allowing the writing to become a mosaic from a Jahweh historian, called "J," in the era of David or Solomon, edited further by Elohist priest historians during the exile, and finally by a writer called the Deuteronomist, who wrote from the northern kingdom after the exile to call the Davidic empire back to a second reading of the law (*deutero*) and a proper observation of the Sinai covenant.

During the modern era, two schools developed, one a maximalist school, counting the history to be true as written, and another a minimalist school, doubting the historical antecedents so far as to claim there was no grand exodus from Egypt of a million Israelites, no fall of Jericho's walls in the time of Joshua, and no occupation of Palestine that eventuated in David's empire. To the early history told by the Jahweh historian, the priestly interpretation of deeply buried memories was added: God's appearance to Abraham, the threat to Isaac, God's wrestling with Jacob, and the ever imponderable scenes at Sinai when the law was given, a law much like what Abraham's antecedents in Sumeria then treated as God's word and intention. At Sinai, the people bowed before fire and earthquake, and yet Moses and the twenty-four elders were invited to come up and eat.

The New Testament generally is not treated to this same analysis; it is usually seen as historical reporting according to the dictates of the first century, which attributed the writing to known personages to gain credence—the disciples authoring the Gospels, Paul writing all his letters—much as the Torah has been attributed to Moses. In this respect, the Matthew and Luke prologues are treated as history.

My contention is that just as the priests in Babylon embroidered the Jahwist story with memories of God's visitations to Abraham and Jacob and Moses, memories explaining how to approach a holy God through temple worship and sacrifice, so too did the "priest" evangelists and theologians (Paul, the writer to the Hebrews, and chiefly James) recast the history of the latter visitation of God in Jesus to tell the story of an imponderable resurrection akin to the appearance at Mount Sinai.

Two of the evangelists (Mark and Matthew) treat the story as a new via media, presenting Jesus as the Lamb of God who takes away the sins of the world when he is sacrificed. Luke, the third evangelist, does not present the death of Jesus as atonement for sin; his gospel lacks any parallel with Matthew and Mark, who call the death a ransom. When Luke follows his gospel with the Acts, Jesus' death is for the forgiveness of sin, but never by sacrifice. The fourth evangelist understands Jesus to be the replacement of the temple in whom we find our life and being, lifted up as was the snake in the wilderness. The body and blood are a symbol for entering into Jesus' life and purpose. There is no priest mediator; the veil has been rent. He was a reality the world had to crucify.

Many Christians make the mistake of believing that the New Testament has replaced the Old and invalidated it, except perhaps for the Old Testament's justification of war and the prophecies they believe are fulfilled by the New and the sexual proscriptions they choose to honor while ignoring health prescriptions.

In order to understand the New Testament, we need to understand the Hebrew Scriptures. The story found there is God's revelation to the Jews while they were in exile—a story different from their captors' beliefs—of a God who has created them and come to them again and again in person, in seasons of following and faithlessness.

As Jesus' followers continue the story, Jesus is the perfect continuation of God's coming to their ancestors and now to them; he is the *shekinah* glory of their temple, tenting with them. Kendall Soulen says: "In the wake of the resurrection the new thing is the Church, the table fellowship of Jews and Gentiles, that prays in Jesus' name for the coming of God's reign. The gospel summons everyone not to cease being Jews or Gentiles, but to glorify the present and future victory of the God of Israel through conformity to Jesus' own solidarity with the other" (page 168).

A mistake is made, however, if we too easily see the New Testament writers simply completing Hebrew Scripture themes. According to their understanding in the first century, Jesus could be equated to the son born to a young woman in Isaiah 14. Likewise, in picking the theme of sacrifice from their tradition and wedding it to the forgiveness of sin (which it was not wedded to in the Hebrew Scriptures), the New Testament writers, excepting John, make the Last Supper into a sacrifice that Jesus' meals did not have or intend. I attribute this to the ascendance of James, the brother of Jesus, who sought to restore a priestly, Levitical, approach to God. The consequence for the church is monumental.

Jesus, revealed as the Son of God at his resurrection, picnics with his disciples by Galilee as Moses and the four and twenty elders picnicked with God at Mount Sinai. The gospel writers get that completed theme right.

To see a bridge between Old and New Testaments, Isaiah 14 to Matthew 1, one needs to know that there has been a long controversy over whether Isaiah was prophesying Jesus' birth. Was his prophecy of a virgin or a young woman? Isaiah tells King Ahaz that a young woman would conceive and that the danger presented by his Assyrian enemies would be dissolved by the time the child came to discernment. The child was a sign of God's presence among them, a promise they needed to trust right then, not four hundred years later. It was a promise Ahaz could not accept or trust. Isaiah's call was to his people to be a suffering servant; it was a lesson for his day on how they were to live. Matthew picked up the promise in the way history was understood in his day and found it to support his theology of Jesus the Messiah, born of a virgin. We can still find a blessing in God's proactive presence among us, Immanuel. Ahaz was to trust that the child represented God's promise of a future.

Absent the prologues to the gospels of Matthew and Luke, our understanding of Jesus as our Lord and Savior would not be different in fact. Those who did not know the story owned him as Lord and Savior, as did those who knew the stories.

Have we factored the effect of these stories and our approach to them into our belief about the Communion elements? No, but they do affect our understanding of bread and wine. If Jesus is the incarnation of God, the argument goes, then the oneness he claimed with the Father and his statements, "this is my body" and "this is my blood," make the elements become his physical presence with us. The better argument is that in his incarnation and life, Jesus shows us how God wishes us to act. He is present to us in the Communion service in the breaking of bread.

Willi Marxsen makes the point that in Jesus' ministry, it is not Jesus, his quality, his being, or his place in relation to God that matters; it is his function of bringing people to God. In this function, there is the possibility to experience God and to anticipate the future now. Function, not being, is key. Action becomes the object of reflection; out of action comes an assertion about him from whom the action derives. So, Marxsen says, it is the cup that is passed around, not the element, not the contents of the cup, but the sharing of the cup, the action, which is important. It is the sharing of the bread that makes us a community. "Because there is one bread, we, who are many, are one body, for we all partake of the one bread" (1 Corinthians 10:17).

This is one point of view, the first thread of the meaning of who Jesus was. It is one way of understanding how to approach the story.

In the next chapter, we will turn to the question, "How did Jesus' death save?"

Odyssey

Taught to be suspicious of all things "liberal," and especially of scholars like Albert Schweitzer, I was moved in seminary to find his testimony about Jesus:

> He comes to us as One unknown without a name, as of old, by the lakeside; He came to those men who knew him not. He speaks to us the same word: '*Follow thou me!*' and sets us to the tasks which he has to fulfill for our time. He commands.
>
> And to those who obey Him, whether they be wise or simple, He will reveal Himself in the toils, the conflicts, the sufferings which they shall pass through in His fellowship, and, as an ineffable mystery, they shall learn in their own experience Who He is. (page 403)

4: How Did Jesus' Death Save?

A second thread in the believers' understanding greatly affects the church's grasp of the Supper. As the new members of the Way sat around their dining room tables, they had to ask, "How did Jesus' death save?" His meals had been welcoming, but was there something more?

Consider the possible development. Recounting Jesus' meals, prominent place would be given to their simple welcoming fellowship. The stories of Mary and Martha, and Zacchaeus—even the meal with Simon the Pharisee. The meals were the natural result of social care, a way to enjoy one another's presence. Maybe they even served as repayment of a social debt. Hadn't Jesus spoken of repayment in the context of certain social obligations? In these occasions, whatever their invitation or debt, the meals had been a forecast, a promise of the welcoming meal of the eternal welcome. He taught that we shouldn't invite only those who can reciprocate, which was a great boundary for all of us to get over.

Still, another question was beginning to be heard. Should the last meal, held at the time of Passover, have Passover overtones?

Not to move to a yearly Passover celebration; the apostle Paul said, "whenever you eat" (not just on Sundays and not just in church), but was there to be a different focus? Was a different understanding of the meal possible? Voices were suggesting themes of repentance and sacrifice. Did Passover suggest a different focus?

Believers began to think about the history of Passover and how they should relate to its meaning.

Passover's story was older than their recorded history. Rooted in a time of spring-cleaning, it was a time of getting rid of the old leaven, sweeping out the dusty corners, beginning anew. No doubt there was some understanding of the healthiness of doing this; in that sense, it was life affirming. Later, it became a celebration of the flight from Egypt, another new beginning and another sweeping out of the dust of enslavement. With bitter herbs, it recalled suffering; with unleavened bread, the bread of hurried flight; with the promise of "next year in Jerusalem," an invitation to the future, to the new.

After the exile, Passover would lose its joyful, forward-looking character and become a time of sacrifice for the forgiveness of sins in line with the Leviticus story of how to approach God. Instead of a festival of welcoming God's invitation to new life, it became a time of atonement for being fundamentally at odds with God, looking back, and longing for the leeks of Egypt.

Was the last meal with the living Jesus to be understood in this new light? Sitting around their tables, welcoming neighbors, how did repentance at a meal fit with the story of Zaccahaeus? Didn't he repent afterward? When guests were invited, was it a time of storytelling? When it was just family, was it a Passover of regret? Was the call to the future muted?

This is what we know outside the New Testament account: Putting it together, they remembered that during the long years before Jesus came, a strong connection began to be made between the sacrifice of Isaac and the Passover, principally in the Book of Jubilees. This connection had become the view held by the Jewish imagination during Jesus' day. This is the influence of tradition of which we spoke at the beginning of the last chapter; this influence would begin to affect the understanding of the Supper, especially as a sense of guilt began to pervade believers' lives (as it had in the Leviticus experience of their forebears).

Our traditional understanding of Isaac makes him a passive, weak figure in the story of Abraham, who was ordered to sacrifice him. If one reads between the lines of that story, however, some problems with passivity develop. The chief problem is that Isaac's age is never disclosed, and we are puzzled: how old was he, and what happened to him in this strange experience? Jewish scholars speculated that he was any of several various ages: fourteen, twenty-five, or thirty-seven; the last being his age if the immediate break in the text suggests that the threat of sacrifice caused Sarah's death. He was born when she was ninety, and she died at 127 years. Did the threat of sacrifice kill her? What would be your response if your husband said, "God says to kill our son?"

Any choice—fourteen, twenty-five, or thirty-seven—has to make one wonder what it all meant to Isaac. Some argue that Isaac, at any of these ages, was not passive but complicit in his desire to serve Abraham's God. He takes Abraham's hand and walks with him. Middle Eastern men of some age still take each other's hands as they walk. Think Saudi Crown Prince Abdullah and George Bush. Think complicity! The Book of Jubilees salutes Isaac.

Isaac becomes a Christ figure by his choice; he becomes an archetypal salvation figure, the lamb led to slaughter, the sheep before his shearers, dumb. The record of his life is passed over with little comment, few of his words recorded. When Abraham's servant brings him a wife, he is wandering Walt Whitman-like in the fields. With some irony, the ram that saves him on the mount will appear again in the ram Rachel uses to shear Esau of his patrimony.

He will live out his days, not in Beersheba with his father (alienated?), but at Beer-lahai-roi (meaning "Thou God seest me") with Ishmael, where Hagar saw a well, and from where they will travel together, Ishmael and Isaac, to bury Abraham at Hebron. His experience will never again be directly mentioned in Hebrew Scripture. He's the forgotten man. But lamb led to the slaughter, sheep dumb before its shearer, he seems a Christ figure and a symbolic invitation to our world of Christian-Muslim conflict for the children of Abraham to travel together.

In the popular imagination of Jesus' day, witnessed in the Book of the Jubilees but without biblical warrant or citation, it is this Isaac, saved by the blood of a ram, who becomes the sacrificial lamb. His importance grows so that the New Testament will open with Jesus saluted as the Lamb of God—popularly, if not scripturally, a second Isaac. It is this lamb in the day's popular religious understanding that is sacrificed at the Passover. The young Christians would come to adopt this understanding. John the Baptist hails Jesus as the Lamb of God. The apostle Paul will carry forward the theme of God's sacrifice of Jesus, calling him our paschal lamb (1 Corinthians 5:7).

Forgiveness is added to the Passover theme in the gospel account, a theme Passover did not originally have, because it had come to be so understood in that day. Originally, Passover had the theme of joyful release, purchased at cost, but filled with promise. Mixed with penitence during the wilderness experience, its theme had changed and would change their understanding of the Last Supper Jesus had with his disciples, called a *chaburah*, into a meal with the heavy repentance theme we have come to know so well. Repentance becomes the welcoming card to the supper. This, against the storyline in which repentance *results* from meals with Jesus—again, consider Zacchaeus who eats, then repents.

Yes, the Last Supper was a celebration of Passover, not because of Passover, but because it occurred at Passover time. Passover signified the peoples' release from servitude in Egypt and would therefore celebrate the worshiping community's release from its various servitudes. This was a joyful template of Passover—replacing the old leaven, starting anew. Jesus was inviting the disciples to this journey with him into resurrection life.

The new journey, the escape from the old enslavements of Egypt combined with a sacrifice for sin as tradition developed. "Christ our paschal lamb" in the apostle Paul's writing reflects this character of sacrifice. Later interpretation made Passover *only* a sacrifice for sin. The Lamb's blood would be spattered against the "lintels of the doors of their lives," and God's angel of destruction would pass over them.

How sacrifice entered Paul's thinking may be attributed to popular religious imagination; or his understanding was the result of the time he spent with James after his Damascus Road experience. The idea of sacrifice was useful as he sought to correct a perversion of the "eating with Jesus" theme that had occurred in Corinth. This correction occurred in the fifties (CE) without any word of the Last Supper being about the forgiveness of sin. The Synoptic Gospels, written some twenty years later, will treat this interpretation as original to the time of Jesus' last meal (Matthew 26:28), confusing all of us.

In all probability, this was Paul's own "re-writing" of tradition since John does not treat it in this manner in his gospel, having written even later. Paul's understanding of the Supper says nothing about the forgiveness of sins; anything reformative is about care for the body of believers. How would these Corinthians have understood a responsibility for this death or their guilt for its perpetration? Paul's complaint is that they have not been discerning of the body, the family—they have not been welcoming—and, thus, they have not represented the heavenly welcome.

So, let's continue to choose the joyous fellowship-supper-with-Jesus theme over the "eating Jesus" or forgiveness of sins theme common today. Forgiveness of sin is granted us not in and through the elements but as we preach Christ crucified for us.

To this day there is a great divide. The greater part of the church, Orthodox, Catholic, and Reformed, chooses to close the circle and elevate the elements of the meal. A few choose the symbolic action of breaking and eating, welcoming family and outsider alike. The Salvation Army and our Friends, the Quakers, choose to do neither of these. The Protestant wing to which I belong, sometimes called the Free Church, subtly, apologetically, bows to the elements side of the argument and, with it, the rarity and heaviness of its celebration, sometimes theorizing about what taking the sacrament can do for you: improve your character and spirituality. Blocking children, unbelievers, and even those not of the same kosher understanding makes the sacrament an issue of essence rather than action. So we search for the manger and miss the incarnation found in living out the supper.

We have noted that originally Jesus' humanity was uppermost in the Christian's confession. John sets it strikingly: "We declare to you what was from the beginning, what we heard, what we have seen with our eyes, what we have looked at and touched with our hands, concerning the bread of life" (1 John 1:1). Even as the creeds began to be formulated, though they ignored the testimony about the way he lived, they were careful to keep the equal division of man and God in Jesus. The issue of the birth was at first important to support that he was a human being, and only later was Mary's virginity used to defend Jesus' godliness.

As the years passed, the argument would center on how this change in the bread and wine occurred. Was the Mass a re-sacrifice of Christ upon the cross or simply a sign of that sacrifice? What is signified by the fact that the Mass is not celebrated on Good Friday? Was that one sacrifice enough for one day? Had Christ's death once and for all freed us from sin, or was the Mass a necessary application of that sacrifice, without which one could not benefit from the salvation Jesus offered? It was principally over this methodological argument that the Reformation occurred. The continuing issue of essence would remain much the same for the Reformers, particularly for Luther, and even for all Protestants.

Intellectually, we may not accept the transubstantiation of bread and wine, the hair at the nape of our necks may not rise, but the elements may have an emotional hold on us that belies our belief. Augustine still preaches to us. There can be no doubt that the birth narratives contributed to this understanding. Because we have learned to mistrust our own humanity, we give the prologues to the gospels greater weight in thinking of Jesus' divinity and so also the essence of the supper elements.

This hallowing was accomplished not only through Matthew and Luke's birth narratives, but also through what happened in the second century, which subtly underlined the change in doctrine. There was no scheming to bring this about; it happened accidentally. The robing of clergy (which was actually yesterday's way of dressing) caught the imagination: "we are equal to the civil authorities; we are still here." Recycling the basilicas as places of worship made concrete witness to the empire and formalized the believers' worship.

The elements were to be consecrated and were served later only by the bishops and priests. As the second century dawned, a bishop claimed the elements had become the medicine of immortality. Clergy came to represent an order that was disappearing in civic life. The ringing of bells and the dismissal of unbelievers and those still being catechized objectified the elements on the altar. The distancing of the altar and, later, its fencing, elevated the meaning of the bread and wine. Still, Jesus' humanness continued to be a powerful understanding that believers held. He was one of us. Art through the Middle Ages will picture the infant in his mother's arms pointing to his penis. Human and divine strive together as they have through the centuries.

In this struggle, the nature of the bread and wine would be lost—believers would forget that they are the elements of our most basic need and symbols of God's care for us. Gone was the major conception that the meaning of the sacrament was in its action, the action to which it called believers. Its meaning was not in its nature, transformed or not.

In the Middle Ages, there would be cries from the congregation to lift the host higher (in order for a standing congregation to see and, especially, revere it). Bread and wine were being lifted in their holy apartness.

The consequences extended through the turbulent Reformation days to our day, and they still affect our understanding of the nature of the sacrament. Poll any Catholic Christian about the sacrament, poll any evangelical Christian today, and you will find equally that the contents of the cup and bread (though appreciated differently) are of greater importance than the action their passing represents.

Bread and cup are holy, not to be treated casually. Passing chips and grapes to children has always seemed a little off to me; but it is my problem, not those who have understood these elements to represent bread and wine.

In sharing bread and wine, we say that these are the gifts of God, common gifts of everyday life, that speak to the sustenance that all people crave and the sustenance that God wants all people to have. In ways almost inexplicable, they mediate God's presence with us. We understand them as emblems of God's care, signs of creation's goodness and of God's covenant with us. They represent the receiving of life's necessities at God's hand (perhaps that is my problem with chips and grapes), and in that sign of God's help to us, we understand Jesus' words—"This is my body, my blood."

Unfortunately, the long arc of understanding these elements to be transforming into Jesus' actual body and blood has given great power to the transformer priest. In that power, bishops currently seek to prevent politicians who separate their beliefs and their responsibility to the public from coming to the table. Where Jesus invitingly ate with those not keeping the "rules," the rule has become "exclude those who do not keep the rules." But this is not a Protestant denouncement of a Roman Catholic understanding. Deep in the Protestant psyche, this same consideration sets contents of cup apart from action. We do not publicly prevent, but neither do we invite, those who stand apart.

In sum, theorizing about what the sacrament can do for you (shape character, remove your sins) will rest in essence rather than action. The elements then trump action, and moralism and perfection—or what Luther would call "works righteousness"—trump doing.

Here, then, are the early traces that answer our question: what happened? The church turned from a call to openness to the removal of guilt and the sensibility of safety. Believers saw what openness had caused their forebears. They were cut off from their land, their patrimony. To remain pure, believers felt they must fence the table. If they let the "wrong" people into their worship or their lives, these people might well turn the believers into the authorities, and they might die—even as their Lord had died.

But believers did not want to envision the irony of that or count on a promised resurrection. Stories of the birth strengthened them, but the stories of his life lost their power to make them open and accepting. Church creeds as early as the beginning of the second century completely ignored a recital of Christ's life. That he freely chose his death became obscured by a picture of a penalizing God.

Furthermore, it was much easier to return to the old ways than to turn again to the freedom of the creation, their new creation, as the good news according to John had called them do. In our experience, we allow the table to have boundaries, too—and not just with regard to who is welcomed to it, but in thinking that Communion only deals with salvation from our sins rather than with the unbound freedom of calling us to live for others.

Odyssey

A Chicago childhood did not open me up to any other Supper practices. We did not visit other churches. Catholic relatives were wrong. We were right. Ours was a memorial service, not a re-enactment of Jesus' sacrifice on the cross. In our churches, there were no crosses; we were churches of the open tomb (with a kind of tomb mentality).

My Communion experience was lower keyed than a friend's Buena Memorial Presbyterian Church service: each Communion cup was a small silver chalice. The elders moved in stately stance. There, we did not move into alternating rows. There were no Bible verses; just silence.

At Princeton (where there was a gold cross on every Communion table), I did not deal with any of the issues that would later occupy me: I was anxious about memorizing the correct words, the pauses, and the gestures for the practicum, not with trying to grasp deeper dimensions. Gestures were big. I learned doctrines, such as transubstantiation, words like sacrament, rather than ordinance. I was not touched by, nor I think taught, anything the least mystical. Had not Calvin said that the church is present wherever the gospel is truly heard and the sacraments rightly administered?

All was correct administration. We were told that small groups, or youth groups we might lead, should not celebrate Communion. The logic was that the whole body of Christ needs to be present, the whole church. Here again, the bishop in charge of elements made holy by his blessing, pastor as pontiff.

Entering the pastorate, I administered as I had been taught.

5: Did Jesus Die For Our Sins?

There are seven considerations to take into account when answering whether Jesus died for our sins.

1. The Historical Account

Why did Jesus die? Jesus died at the hands of the Roman government for upsetting the status quo in one of its provinces. He had challenged his people, as had the prophets before him, to accept the claims of God's realm, especially its care for the poor in a debtor economy and its evangelical welcoming and love for insider and outsider alike. His religious community was upset, fearing the Roman hegemony and his different ideas.

His message threatened the Roman government, as he talked of another kingdom. The pageantry of Jesus' entry into Jerusalem provoked political fears; a blind beggar hailed him as the son of David, an appellation that was political, not just religious. Thousands, says the account, crowded around him. Imagine the consternation that would arouse.

His message, contrary to his peoples' understanding of purity and oneness and its consequent kosher arrangements, disturbed the people. It was upsetting to hear that all were welcome to a great banquet of life and that keeping your arrangement of eating only with your own did not make you God's favorites as you had assumed. Some of us assume this to this day.

Shaping its story, the young church recalled Jesus' welcoming ways, eating with people they disliked, such as the tax collector, Zacchaeus; people they feared, such as the revolutionary zealot Judas Iscariot; people they were uncomfortable with, such as the sick, the poor, and women; and people they considered enemies, such as Romans and Samaritans. Jesus' welcoming ways convinced them that they were guilty of being self-centered. These stories fill the Gospels. Imagine our telling our story this way!

It is interesting that the stories of eating in the Acts and in the Apostle Paul's accounts have nothing to say of forgiveness of sins. Meals are welcoming and thus offering the welcome of forgiveness.

2. Reformulating the Historical Account

To say that the young church "shaped" its understanding of Jesus, requires understanding various levels of Scripture interpretation. The literal sense may not be literal. Mark "shaped" his materials for a Gentile audience, and John re-worked timetables, events, and meanings.

We have greater difficulty understanding that the gospel writers shaped their remembrance of Jesus' exact words. Did he say exactly this, or are his words written just as they understood them?

Is the inspiration of Scripture, its words, the exact words of God, or do they just represent God's intentions? If the latter, in what ways do we trust the words? We trust them in ways that the Spirit authenticates them in the church's corporate life, past and present. In that corporate life, a different understanding came to shape the meal, and ideas about sin could be challenged.

3. What changed?

Receiving the story, believers shifted its primary focus from the kingdom of God drawing near because that could be understood to challenge political authority. They did this for their own safety in a day that demanded that Caesar be sworn as Lord. Their understanding of the message called them to care and protect the poor and downtrodden. They would do so without a political edge that might threaten their ability to do that.

Under James's influence (as I argue elsewhere), the young church focused on the meaning of Christ's death for their failures (sin). Though sacrifice in their Hebrew Scriptures had not originally been for the atonement of sin, they now understood his death on the cross to be such an atonement. They came to understand his Last Supper as an introduction to that atonement, unlike the meals they had regularly shared with him and unlike meals that he told them to accept when they were out on a mission. After the resurrection, old ideas needed re-thinking.

The focus of their meals soon became on how the meal mediates forgiveness. Again, this change is not recorded in the scriptural account. We know it only through tradition.

The Gospels do not report this as a change in focus. The Synoptics say that the Last Supper was a Passover meal, and only Matthew describes it as being for the forgiveness of sin. John contends it was a meal before Passover and then does not describe the meal in order to focus instead on the welcoming act of foot washing.

Paul shows the meal to be a welcoming act and says nothing about the forgiveness of sins, not even in what "he has received from the Lord and handed on" to them. The Corinthians failed to be welcoming. When Paul speaks of tradition, he is speaking of the sacrifice tradition he received from James. When he says Jesus was handed over to death for our trespasses and raised for our justification, he is not addressing the Supper.

There is no dispute that the meal had Passover themes. It was Passover. The dispute is whether these themes are for the forgiveness for sins (Matthew is alone in his interpretation), or an invitation to join Jesus in an exodus to new life, the new life his meals had signified.

4. Development of the Meaning of Passover

Passover's meaning developed from a Sumerian spring festival for getting rid of old leaven and making a fresh start. It became an invitation to another kind of fresh start and new life when the Israelites were called out of Egypt, the call coming at great price, including the death of Egyptian firstborns and the death of a lamb to protect their own firstborns against the threat of death. For Jews, Passover remains a call to new life today: "Next year in Jerusalem!" The importance of sacrifice in reaching the challenge of a new day is not denied during Passover, but the meal is certainly not focused on forgiveness. Pentecost will pick up on this understanding.

The idea of forgiveness began to take hold in the common mind as the meaning of the sacrifice of a lamb was reflected upon. There was no biblical storyline involving forgiveness in the festival itself. Even today in Judaism forgiveness is sought in a Day of Atonement. But a growing consensus (Jubilees 4) by Jesus' time conflated forgiveness and a new start in the Passover celebration ("Behold the Lamb of God, who takes away the sins of the world"). There is no lamb on the menu of the last meal Jesus shared with his disciples. Why would this have been omitted in the retelling of a meal the disciples were sent to prepare? Jesus becomes the lamb slain for us on the cross before the foundation of the world in the church's tradition. But for John, "This is my body" (bread) and "This is my blood" (wine) were enough.

5. Understanding Sin

The development of the concept of sin began with the story of the first parents breaking faith with God's instruction. Theology calls this the fall; the story does not. The Yahwist author tells the story (perhaps sparked by David's sin), as it exemplifies graphically the origin of Israel's wish to be independent from God. The story is a paradigm describing sin as a desire to be independent, and from this desire all breaking of the covenant and its commandments follows.

Paul speaks of Jesus and sin in various ways. He says while we were yet sinners, Christ died for us; he died for our sins, became sin for us. From Augustine to Calvin, the meaning of this is contested. We are also told that Christ was without sin, so Paul suggests that Christ became a sin offering, not that he committed sin; God put Christ in our place so that we might stand in Christ's place. All of these are theological formulations built upon the tradition of sacrifice.

Believing that original sin developed after the biblical story of

Adam and Eve and the psalmist's "I was born guilty, a sinner when my mother conceived me" (51:5) and that it was solved only by Jesus' death on the cross is contradicted by the psalmist's "wash me" and Isaiah's "What to me is the multitude of your sacrifices … wash yourselves, do good, seek justice" (Psalm 51:2; Isaiah 1:11, 16–17). This belief was picked up again in the Baptists' baptism for the forgiveness of sin.

Jesus participated in that baptism to identify with those he came to. Paul's understanding was that "God made him sin who knew no sin so that in him we might become the righteousness of God" (2 Corinthians 5:21).

To say "Jesus died for our sins" is to understand that we are complicit in rejecting the love that the world could not abide. We, too, want to be free to center on ourselves and on the now rather than the eternal. From that desire we may be washed.

6. Atonement

Originally, atonement was meant to present the worshiper as holy before God through the sacrifice of a pure animal or bird or an offering of grain at the altar of the Tabernacle; these acts removed the slight of insensitivity to God's holiness. This practice is witnessed to by the Muslim custom of washing feet before entering the mosque. Symbolically, the mind is focused on God; not the affairs of the day. The Israelite likewise came before God. For the Christian, the onus of our responsibility is removed as Jesus becomes the pure sacrifice, covering our inadequacy and perhaps making us too casual about appearing before God.

From the beginning, atonement only covered unwitting sin, ignorance of a commandment's demand, or some change in the body (a woman's flowering [KJV], a man's emission or rash), some evidence of uncleanness as it was thought of or a lack of wholeness in oneself. In everything, worshipers were to be one as God is one.

No atonement for intentional sin meant death or expulsion from the tribe. This understanding of sin and its atonement was developed years after Israel's story began. It was told in the exile as if it were understood from the beginning in order to educate the people and keep them faithful. It evidently did not hold for David, who was forgiven his sin with Bathsheba, but the theorizing of some scholars sees a Yahwist footprint in David's story: Israel's history is told as a way to understand David's failure.

The root of forgiveness for intentional sin may be found in the story of Phineas, who thrusts his spear through the abdomens of an Israelite and Moabite woman in the act of coitus when the people sinned by worshipping Baal at Peor—a sacrifice of one for the many. From this root grew a history of believing violence was necessary for forgiveness.

Jesus said that only one sin is unforgivable, the sin against the Holy Spirit. Apparently this means a refusal to be visited by the Eternal, or things eternal, thus blocking any communication. The letter to the Hebrews says that if we willingly persist in sin after having received the word of truth, there no longer remains a sacrifice for sin. The church has not always accepted this.

Simultaneously, with the codification of the law, wisdom literature developed a system of forgiveness apart from the sacrificial system that involved intentional purity of the heart (see Psalm 15 and the prophets' discounting of sacrifice), and forgiveness was then found in suffering and washing (baptism or the purging with hyssop).

When the New Testament opens, the apparent common understanding is that atonement for sin is possible through baptism and sacrifice ("Behold the Lamb of God who takes away the sin of the world").

7. Forgiveness

Forgiveness is available to us if we repent, if "we turn around," "come to ourselves," and believe. This understanding is based on scriptural stories and injunctions we have known from childhood, apart from taking Communion. The reason is that Jesus mediated forgiveness to seekers in his life, his ministry. Jesus showed that forgiveness should be given apart from his death and without previous observable repentance (the woman "taken in sin"; Zacchaeus).

The Question

Did Jesus die for our sins? This is the church's understanding, which has come down to us based on James's tradition, based on gratitude for Jesus' death and a commitment to keeping the idea of sacrifice in the new covenant from the former covenant. Corinthian believers would not have understood a charge that they had caused Jesus' death, so Paul framed the issue of the supper in terms of their not honoring the body of believers.

The Answer

Jesus died for our sins, allows us to find forgiveness in his death, to be "covered" by his blood. This is valid, but it is only one understanding, a church tradition understanding. It has at times led to a kind of individualism unknown to the first century ("I come to the garden alone") and a contentment with one's salvation that may not spur us to live as Christ lived.

In truth, the death was the result of Roman action. Jesus understood his mission, message, and ministry as a paradigm of God's gracious forgiveness to us. He understood this to be justly walking with God. He understood that the world could not understand or accept a love like his and that living out such love would lead to his death. The world cannot accept judging itself in such a mirror. It prefers that one must die for the many.

Jesus died at the hands of the Roman government. We are called to live as he lived. To accept that may lead to death, but also it may lead us to the eternal banquet Jesus invites us to. It removes the blame so often put upon the Jews and thus the resulting history of anti-Semitism that is the shame of the "Christian" world. It also saves us from theorizing about whether God sacrificed his son or was abusive, bargained with the devil, paid a ransom, or is a contributing factor in the justification of violence.

Jesus is not just the moral example we are to follow. The death still requires us to appreciate that it is like no other. Understanding that is to understand how Jesus has brought our world into the balance that God saw at creation. Or, as Paul put it, that Jesus is

God's *yes*. It is not just a construct of our belief; it is God who has welcomed us home. This welcome is from the foundation of the world and beyond any power of reason.

To some, this approach is accused of being noetic, an approach that has enabled the church to "understand" the saving character of Christ's death. It is not that. It is the autonomous act of God.

The reproach that this is Gnosticism, or the belief that one can be saved by knowledge rather than having to admit one is in bondage to sin and in need of divine rescue, is a reproach we may deny. This is no prideful claim that "this is my doing." It is understanding that this is exactly God's doing, God's rescue, a painful but joyful coming to the self that it is not I, but God, and God does not need blood sacrifice to bring us to God's self. This approach is the prophets' "what is required of you is not the blood of lambs, the blood of the firstborn."

Excursus: A Brief Look at Leviticus

If I return to Leviticus, it is because I consider it a pivotal book in our understanding of Christian faith. I have been interested in the book of Leviticus since my first year in seminary, when my Bible professor, Howard Tillman Kuist, told us it was the Federal Health Administration (FHA) manual of its day!

But Leviticus is more than that; it is a central book in Jewish life. The letter to the Hebrews shows most clearly the struggle of the young church to understand the Leviticus commandments; one of these Jesus cites as the second law: You shall love your neighbor as yourself (19:18). Jesus was schooled in it. Lately, the church has not valued its other commandments much, except its prohibition of homosexual acts.

How does Leviticus affect our understanding of Holy Communion?

Upon the escape from Egypt as told in Exodus, God commands a tabernacle be erected for worship to house the ark of the covenant. An altar of sacrifice was to be placed before it, and then the book describes the worship that was meant to happen there. The book does not cite Moses as its author, though its repeated assertions that the Lord spoke to Moses may suggest that to the reader. Its ancient materials are believed to have been assembled during the exile by the priests.

But remember its original setting: various commandments were given because certain animals were sacred to Canaanite deities, and certain practices (homosexual relations) were prohibited because the devotees of Baal practiced them. Health was placed in the context of holiness so that the people would endure.

It was a way of theologizing. Those who assembled the book wanted to show that God was one (no mixed cloth or crops in a field) and holy, separating themselves from others to show their holy apartness. So, they were to live a life that provided witness to this oneness.

What did this mean to the people of the exile who could not worship as commanded? What did the writers of the New Testament appreciate? We have noted Jesus' citation of the second law, and "Be holy as the Lord your God is holy," would also have resonated. The question of holy and common, clean and unclean, appears in the Gospels as well.

Leviticus is divided into four sections: guidelines for spontaneous sacrifices, services in the sanctuary, practical holiness, and gifts to the sanctuary. The first of these is pertinent to our discussion here. How does one approach God if one has unwittingly broken a commandment or a bodily function has made one unclean? One may not approach if one's sin is intentional; its consequence is death or separation from the tribe. The remedy for intentional sin is not given until the wisdom tradition of the Psalms.

How often might such sacrificial approaches have been made? Consider it: some four hundred thousand adult campers, according to the story, and one tabernacle. What availability of sacrificial animals would there have been in an absolutely barren wilderness where there was no meat other than quail? Was this a mythical sacrificial system?

Leviticus challenges us to ask what lessons may be drawn from the fact that the priestly writers in Babylon wanted to remind their people of God's requirements for worship. The tabernacle altar was no longer available. Why would it be that unintentional sins could be atoned for, but intentional sin would be met with death or expulsion? Nothing is said about one's interior response to sacrifice as we find in today's services (no *mea culpa*); the blood was spattered on the altar—sometimes on the people. The Psalms plead for a clean heart. But is this interiority defined by our own Romantic period rather than what the ancients may have perceived?

The New Testament has no book of Leviticus, though the letter to the Hebrews comes close. And although sin and atonement are important themes in the New Testament, it does not provide us with any actions for gaining atonement. Paul echoes Isaiah in this more personal approach, saying, "Since all have sinned and fall short of God's glory, they are now justified by his grace as a gift through the redemption that is in Christ Jesus, whom God put forward as a sacrifice through the redemption by his blood, effective through faith" (Romans 3:23–25). In Paul we have a melding of sacrifice for sin and Passover (Christ being our Passover), as these themes are joined. The way to forgiveness is believing and assenting, but not communing.

Leviticus undeniably would have shaped the young believers' understanding of conduct, but not worship. Jesus had become the tabernacle tenting with them, approachable without sacrifice of animal or bird, without fear of unacceptability, as the woman with the issue of blood proves. The meaning of the Last or Lord's Supper is not hinged on proving yourself. The Supper in its Passover themes looks forward to new life. In Jesus' meals, there was no hint of getting right with God; repentance comes after the meal.

A New Testament understanding of Leviticus is still key for us.

To the good news of John we now turn.

Odyssey

Maundy Thursday "celebrations" become heavy with guilt rather than invitations to a great escape. I admit I didn't know how to change this. Not even the popular practice of combining the celebration with a Seder service removes the temptation to dwell on remorse. The guilt is there—"Is it I?" Take a page from Reform Judaism, whose Passover Seder services speak to bringing a new freedom to the world, a hint of "Next year in Jerusalem!" and William Blake's,

> I will not cease from mental fight
> Nor shall my sword sleep in my hand,
> Till we have built Jerusalem
> In England's green and pleasant land.

6: THE GOOD NEWS ACCORDING TO JOHN

As you begin John's gospel, you sense that something different is afoot. The setting, like the book of Genesis, places you in the beginning of the world, and what is created in this new world is life and light as surely as it was at the beginning. But also created are grace and truth, grace and truth that will set you free if you will only eat of the tree of life. The old prohibition of eating its fruit is gone. The fall is undone. This new creation is not of sun and moon or flora and fauna, but of a different way to see and live in the world.

This theme of a new creation organizes John's thoughts. It shapes his perspective as he presents the good news of Jesus in a way quite different from that of his fellow evangelists. Events will occur at different times. Some events, like the Last Supper, will be transformed in keeping with this new creation. John tells his story very forthrightly from the other side of the resurrection, using the resurrection as a motif ("on the third day") more patently, but more mythically, than the other evangelists. The consequences are important.

Billy Graham in years past recommended the gospel of John to new converts for their initiation into faith. Mark has an everydayness that seems more inviting and straight on to the modern mind. I understand that Graham chose John because John presents claims of new birth most clearly. The fact is, however, that this means seeing the Jesus story without the prism of the new creation. With resurrection motifs and a changing chronology, the new convert is presented with a worldview that is quite different. It takes eyes of faith to see all of John's differences and allow for them. Without these eyes of faith, one may succumb to attacks on the credibility of the gospel record.

Witness the marvelous treatment of the materials John had before him. After the prologue, you do not have the story of a birth, but a new birth: the meeting of some men who will be reborn as disciples when they are introduced to Jesus as the Lamb of God who takes away the sin of the world. Their meeting is rather offhanded and cryptic and seemingly counterintuitive to the grand opening. When the disciples inquire where Jesus is staying, he says, "Come and see."

Some suggest that "come and see" is Jesus' invitation to show that he is not staying downtown with the elite absentee landlords, but out in the hedgerows with the poor of the land who are outcast in the eyes of the religious hierarchy because they cannot keep the cleanliness laws. But even if this is only surmised, the invitation is to experience life together in its most open and basic ways. "Live with me." This becomes John's theme: "We declare what was from the beginning, what we've heard ... seen ... touched with our hands" (1 John 1:1).

John has, at any rate, transformed the story Luke opens with. A new day has dawned in Jesus; on the countryside the lowly are tented with, a new *shekinah* glory is here, the very presence of God experienced in the tabernacle of old. The mighty have been deposed. Luke's recording of Mary's Magnificat deposition is being played out in a new strophe, using everyday language and experience. He includes no birth story, but all of Luke's otherworldly glory invades the common life of these disciples; there are no outcast shepherds in their shepherd fields, but he uplifts the common life of fisher folk, outcast accountants, and tax collectors. In a creative stroke, John has made people of different occupations one with the shepherds. He has upset the classical style of making an introduction focus on people of stature. There are no magi, but we are there!

John continues his surprises: Jesus leads these new disciples to a wedding at Cana in Galilee. He casts the wedding in the mystical form of the great wedding banquet of the eschaton by introducing it as a resurrection story occurring *on the third day.* "Follow me," Jesus is saying, "and the wedding banquet of eternity has come today." In this first of the meals that Jesus shares, the meal comes with fine wine beyond measure, just as the prophets of old had predicted. John uses the phrases of the crucifixion and resurrection story to set his account: "on the third day ... woman, my hour has not come"; and he tells us in this first sign that Jesus' glory is revealed and that the disciples believe in him.

But Jesus' invitation is not only to the great banquet. It is to find the banquet in himself—not in his being, but in his life. Where Luke next shows Jesus as a young boy encountering the sages in the temple, John will tell us that Jesus is the temple. He moves the time of the cleansing of the temple to the beginning of his story to set another great theme of this gospel: Jesus has replaced the temple. Using a methodology he often repeats, John has Jesus enter into a discussion that his listeners misunderstand, just as the rabbis were puzzled in their discussion with the young Jesus. His listeners think that Jesus is speaking of the Jerusalem temple from which he has just driven the money changers. But he is speaking of his own body, which does the Father's will.

Then he cleanses the temple: the act that the other gospels will say costs him his life, upsetting a détente that had kept the Romans out of the temple as long as there was no civil unrest. John sees the conflict caused instead by the raising of Lazarus, an act that salutes God's power in the world and acts as a direct challenge to Rome's hegemony. Bringing Lazarus back to life, says John, caused Jesus' death. The fruit of the tree is eaten; death has been denied. The world cannot abide such a vision.

And so John's story continues the transformation to a new creation. Jesus becomes the temple. Where the other gospels hold back on discussing Jesus' meaning for life, John places the witness at the second Passover when he feeds the thousands. He depicts a Eucharist-like scene. Then just before the third Passover of his ministry, something strange happens at the Last Supper. We look for the liturgy or the menu, and we do not find them. Instead we find

John revisiting the meaning of Passover, a new trek to the Promised Land. Menu and liturgy is replaced; the way forward is through the washing of feet.

To find the Supper's liturgy, we have to skip back in the story to that second Passover some chapters earlier in which Jesus explains that being one with him, eating body and blood, is to do his Father's will. New manna is here. Manna fed thousands in the exodus: here, five thousand adults and others are fed.

Then to the dismay of some latter day readers, a different dating and meaning of the crucifixion upsets the apple cart. This new setting and direction are critical for understanding that the Last Supper was not meant to be associated with themes only of sacrifice and atonement. Passover for John is the flight from old captivities through wilderness to new life. Jesus was showing the power of his example for daily living and for salvation through the daily breaking of bread, drinking, and washing feet. His regular suppers with the disciples became a Last Supper. He was not building a theology for the Mass.

Passover and exodus and even exile are a daily, revolutionary way of living at the table, in business dealings, in home life, and in synagogue. In a rigid, stratified society, this view would come like an explosion. Hey! In our secularized, accommodationist, and assimilated day, templates of Passover, exodus, and exile do not particularly speak to us, and so we miss the revolution!

A critical challenge for our understanding is to see the difference between the final supper and the Lord's Supper. The final supper is the meal Jesus invited his disciples to share with him during the Passover time before his death. The controversy becomes whether this was a regular meal or what would become the Lord's Supper in church nomenclature. Some have suggested that this was a *chaburah*, an evening supper he had been regularly sharing with them, a meal that celebrates family or friends, banding them together in special fellowship somewhat like the house churches in some of our congregations or the Methodist classes instituted by John Wesley.

In these chaburahs, family, children, and friends took part. At this chaburah, just before the time they would regularly celebrate a Passover Seder, we overhear a typical bit of conversation as Jesus talks about himself and his Father's will. The meal is both normal and special on this last occasion of eating together. It is later church history that makes the meal a ritual that crystallizes what we do.

The words *body* and *blood*, not found in John at the supper but in that earlier discourse, are not institutional words, as will develop when the final supper becomes the Lord's Supper. The institutional words will not become a part of the agape and supper fellowships of the young church until well into the second century, even though they appear in the Synoptic Gospels. The words did not become a mandated part of the liturgy until the twelfth century and Peter Lombard. These institutional words are what are so misunderstood in what has become the Lord's Supper. Jesus is calling for action, not a salute to his being. We are to act as he acted. This is not just *us* invited to supper. We are inviting the world to the banquet! And this is the truth that makes what has happened to the supper so amazing.

John understands body and blood as being one in will and purpose with Jesus, as Jesus has said he is with God. There are Passover themes because it is Passover, but in the telling for our day, it is not quite a Passover Seder; it is a bit beyond that.

We have noted that words are not there. If we had only John's gospel (as some did), we would have only the story of the foot washing, without words to argue over. In our day, with denominational resources and the Internet, we assume instant communication and formation across the land. Not so in John's day. Various communities would believe and practice the faith in different ways and consider themselves followers of Christ.

Jesus becomes the servant at supper, washing his disciples' feet. His core action is to eat with everyone, friend and foe, "sinner and righteous," and disciples are to do the same. He has lifted up the ancient act of eating, of hosting and serving, as a sign of the covenant of peace from Abraham to Isaiah, and is commending this act as a paradigm for life.

The New Jerusalem, traditionally hoped for in the Seder, is here. Jesus invites the disciples to a new exodus, a new crossing over the red sea to the Promised Land of the kingdom of God. He is not saying, "eat my body" in a literal fashion, but that they are to do as he has done.

Something changed. As we saw in the last chapter, the change caused churchly ritual to be substituted for the daily significance of eating at the table some time late in the first century. Did the old Levitical ways suggest something was missing? Was there fear that they might be exiled like their forebears?

John's prayer formula of lifting the hands and looking to heaven, the faithful formula of Jesus' daily meals, was actually his family tradition of faith (we can imagine his mother's action at meals), and it became interpreted in the feeding of the thousands as an early account, or preview, of the Eucharist, the ritual of Communion worship that later developed.

Resonances with the final supper are present in the telling of the feedings. Jesus lifts his eyes to heaven, blesses, breaks, and distributes the bread, a story appropriate to what was happening in the homes of the young Christians in Acts: families, sitting around tables, were telling the stories of Jesus, lifting their eyes, breaking bread, and experiencing the meaning of Jesus' actions in their lives.

It was not what happened one hundred years later in the formalization of worship that caused the feeding stories to take the form of the Eucharist. Eucharist, thanksgiving, is as appropriate to the setting around tables in the homes of the first believers as it is to ritualization. Truly, ritual grows out of the deepest meanings we find in our common lives.

What might be more assuring to persecuted believers in Jerusalem apartments, windows shuttered, doors locked, than to join in the recognition that one day they would be part of all of those gathered on the hillsides? How could they not rejoice in the words of Jesus, "Gather up the fragments that are left over so that nothing will perish"? It is in response to the depth of such a promise that ritual is born. The second century *Didache* has this prayer, which sums up its meaning: "We give thanks to you, our Father ... as this fragmented bread was scattered on the mountains but gathered up and become one, so let the church be gathered from the four corners of the earth into your kingdom."

We are lifted into the solemn fellowship of early Christians around their dining room tables before "church" became an ecclesiastical construct of history, our families and assemblies meeting as the early believers did in the Corinth of the first century, praying for a spiritual reality deeper than any human hunger.

John's setting of the feeding of the thousands in his second Passover time widened the horizons of the Eucharist of the second, third, ninth, sixteenth, or twenty-first centuries. The supper in his telling is a template for the feedings and the fellowship meals of the young church. Ancient Passover, a greater exodus, becomes their calling. Passover was not a thing of timing, or they would have celebrated the supper only annually. Passover became the disciples' way of life. Escape from Egypt was a metaphor for escape from numberless captivities.

Retelling the story of the feeding, John snares us: he says the disciples recalled that it had ended in a strange trip across the Sea of Galilee on a stormy night. In danger of their sinking, Jesus had met them on the sea and brought them safely to shore. How like Jesus to do that! Were the disciples mesmerized by the Exodus story of a Red Sea crossing, or was it really happening? How like our own associations with past events. Their ancestors recalled being safe from the storming Egyptians behind them, so Jesus had come to them, and so he would come again to the turbulent seas of their present persecution. Even today we sing Cecil F. Alexander's 1852 song,

> Jesus calls us o'er the tumult
> of our life's wild restless sea,
> day by day his clear voice
> sounding, saying, "Christian, follow me."

The story, says John, was a sign of God's ever-continuing presence with them, feeding them anew on the hillsides and at their tables and sustaining them as once they had been fed manna in the wilderness. They prayed as they normally prayed, eyes lifted to heaven, offering prayers that would later shape the Eucharist.

Naturally, the crowd on that Galilean hillside had wanted to make Jesus king. Indeed, he was and is King Jesus. And if he was King Jesus and the manna that had come down from heaven, the bread of life to them, then the disciples understood that doing his will and entering into his life of sacrifice were life and blood to them, just as he had tried to make clear. Eating his flesh and drinking his blood were not cannibalism as their adversaries charged but a metaphor for entering deeply into his life and living as he lived, every day.

These stories of Jesus' eating with outsiders and sinners, feeding the thousands, sending the disciples out to eat and stay with whoever would invite them into their homes on their missionary journeys, were understood by early believers as stories meant to programmatically emphasize his message. They were to do likewise. The laws of purity they had upheld in keeping kosher households could no longer fence them away from their neighbors. With these neighbors was the heart of the experience they were beginning to understand as the Lord's Supper. Here, John helped most of all.

John's sources for the timetable of the events of that last week of Jesus' life indicate that the supper was held before Passover. It was a celebration of the open community they had come to know in all their social interactions in Jesus' ministry. It was an invitation to join the next stage of the journey.

While it had repentance overtones, the supper spoke deeply to the facts of life, that community is established only as one's guilt for turning away from community is acknowledged and repented of. While there was sadness, it was in recognition of the fact that we do not always catch on as we might have; they had foreboding fear that something was about to happen that would end their fellowshipping together. They did not, however, have guilt over sin. But the supper, while tense with sorrow, being held before Passover, freed them from concentrating on guilt and sin. They could celebrate the welcoming spirit of openness to life that Jesus had invited them to.

Our mistake is to make the parting sadness of that final supper become the template for our understanding of Communion today, to the exclusion of the invitation to pass over into new life. This was a Passover meal with its ancient mystery of forthcoming adventure and what today's Seders would hail as "next year in Jerusalem!" One need only read the liturgies of today's Reform Judaism's Passovers to see how adventuresome these "passings" to a better world can be; indeed, how political, how just.

In the final meeting before Jesus' crucifixion and in their post-crucifixion reflection on it, everything came together. Eating together had been the hallmark of Jesus' ministry, the ultimate sign of all his signs that this open sense of community was what he was about. It was as ancient and mystical as Abraham's entertaining guests and covenanting with them. It was as present to their day as not forgetting to pay attention to the social amenities of washing a guest's feet. In fact, that simple courtesy showed what community was all about, and its sign of humility was the basis for making community work.

Scholars' arguments over the dating of the Supper are involved. Mark has a Passover meal. John does not make the meal a Passover meal, but it happens on the night when Jesus is handed over to the authorities. The consequence for worship is Passover, not the sacrifice for sins.

John sets the supper before the Passover (chapter 13). Jesus' condemnation and crucifixion take place on the eve of Passover. Jesus dies at the hour when the lambs are slain on the day of preparation, and his body is in the tomb before the Passover begins. This is the high point of John's description of Jesus—"Behold the Lamb of God!" In John's dating, this is Friday, so the next day is the Sabbath. This Sabbath was particularly holy because Passover occurred on the Sabbath. In Mark's dating, the day of Jesus' death had been the Passover, the last meal on the day of preparation. We are hooked by religious colorization.

The Synoptic Gospels take a religiously Jewish tack; John versus Rome. Arguments in favor of John's dating are these: John does not have Jesus' Eucharistic words over the bread and cup. The Passover themes prove no more than that the feast was at hand. Even Mark does not include traditional Passover dishes, though this may be the tradition's re-working to keep Jesus as the lamb. Why is it missing in all the accounts?

If the events leading up to and including the crucifixion are on the eve of Passover, the problem of Simeon coming in from the fields, from work on a holy day, is removed, as are the issues of the religious authorities appearing in Pilate's court on a holy day. The women could buy spices for the preparation for burial, and Joseph of Arimathea and Nicodemus could carry out the burial details.

But of greater importance than these calendar details is the fact that this meeting on the eve of the day of preparation is the apex, the culmination of all that Jesus had wanted to teach his disciples. Graphically, in a symbol, Jesus catches all he has been saying: "If you want to continue my ministry, the best way is to have meals together." And at these meals, wash feet! Welcome others, the outsider, even those who may deny you, who may betray you.

How counter to our religious sensibilities that is! Meals are the sign par excellence that God welcomes everyone to the banquet of life? The meal is not a sacrifice, or a recreation of a sacrifice, as it later became in the Mass? The meal is sign of the way we are to live.

Every day, as easily and regularly as meals take place, this is the way we are to live. There is no ritual according to John, certainly no reservation to a stated day or time, no lofting of the bread or chalice, no fear of spilling the wine, and no denial of these elements to those who are communing lest they be mishandled. Seated at the table are good friends, doubters, questioners, and one who is in the process of making himself an outsider. Yet they commune together.

The meal John portrays may have had overtones of the Passover observance because it is Passover time, but that portrayal does not justify the meal becoming the sacrifice it later became. It was natural in Hebrew history for sacrifice for sin to enter. It was natural for the theme to be there in that week. John captures the essence of the humility that life together requires in portraying the foot washing. All of the themes of Passover deepen the recognition of the human situation that makes communing together vital.

So today, no one at a meal needs to define our captivities or remark about another diner's rescue from alcoholism or the boundedness of frigidity afflicting someone there or the addiction to sexual involvement grasping another or the materialism that binds so many of us. But these captivities are as real to us as any Egyptian sojourn, any Babylonian exile. The acceptance and love that a meal offers invite the overcoming of these destructive habits through crossing over the Jordan to self-esteem, passing through the Samarian boundaries set by our own prejudices, and not evading our own faults or our own complicities in our captivities.

John, like Luke, ends his paean to Jesus' life, death, and resurrection with an account of a meal after the resurrection. It fits all that has gone before. But where Luke lifts up the broken bread and opens the Scriptures, John sings of the reality of life, its need for forgiveness. Jesus again meets the disciples, and the high point of the conversation at that meal is a question to Peter: "Do you love me?"

This is overtly a process question that confronts us all. How do you begin to rebuild the bridges once a break has occurred? Love is the bridge. Jesus' willingness to speak to Peter shows us the way. Instead of avoidance, normal to us, Jesus reaches out. Meals encourage that, but not always. I know our avoidances.

From chapter two to chapter twenty one—and there are arguments for redactors and editors, and we are uncomfortable with his attacks on "the Jews" which must be seen as a response to his church's situation in the late first century, but not excused—John has spun a wise web for the salvation available to us in eating with Jesus and with each other. He has newly created Communion, not just as a supper, but as the experience of following him and identifying his body and blood as the marks of the way we are to live. Many of his listeners misunderstood and departed. The others of us say, "Lord, to whom can we go? You have the words of eternal life." That is the good news with which we welcome one another.

Excursus

How did it happen that the meaning of Passover became associated with the forgiveness of sin?

John is perhaps clearest in disassociating the themes of Passover and the Lord's Supper. He has Jesus host a *last supper* as a testimony to all he has taught about meals. Because it is Passover week, Passover themes are present, including Jesus' saying he had wanted to celebrate the Passover with them. It is John who lifts up Jesus as the Lamb of God. Even Mark has no Passover dishes in his meal (the early church may have tweaked the menu of the new covenant). Was the lack of a full meal a simple omission, something understood without saying, or is it recognition that by the time of the evangelists' writing, the meal had been shaped as a rite to fit their new day?

The question remains, what is the connection that makes Lord's Supper and Mass a time of expiating sin?

The Passover marked Israel's release from Egypt, purchased with the terrible price of Egypt's firstborn and the deaths of the Egyptian forces as they pursued their slaves through the Red Sea. We may grant that enslavement reaps its own consequences: loss of self-worthiness, trust in the captor's superiority. That is difficult to ascribe to God's will. It seems an after-the-fact judgment, a theological construction placed on the event, marked with the saving of Israel's firstborn sons by the splashing of blood on lintel posts. Our present-day judgment is to wonder if we can believe.

Passover is a festival that far preceded the time of Moses; it combined two spring festivals, the agricultural feast of getting rid of household leaven that we see in Exodus 12 and the feast of the slaughter of the firstborn of the flock. These two feasts represent a holistic approach to life: a health measure, understood long before our modern science; getting rid of the old leaven with the resonance of getting rid of old burdens and starting anew; and an act of humble recognition before a greater power that life is a gift.

But a yearly celebration of getting rid of the old and placing one's life in a greater field of meaning may include a parting from one's sins akin to the Prayer Book's, "We do not presume to come to thy Table, trusting in our own righteousness, but in thy manifold and great mercies. We are not worthy. We do not presume." We can say this without being burdened with sin. Jews consider this a marked difference between their faith and that of Christians': their faith is a celebration of the joy and goodness of life, whereas Christians are obsessed with the repentance of sin.

Why was it, then, in this Passover celebration of what was essentially a creation renewal theme in its earliest understanding, that redemption from Egypt should come to be equated with redemption from sin? The Israelites' bondage in Egypt was not of their doing. The later grumbling in the wilderness, the longing for the fleshpots of Egypt, might connote a choosing of slavery rather than freedom, serfdom instead of inheritance. Israel's repeated turning from God, so condemned by the prophets, might well make an argument for needing to be redeemed. But it is neither the wilderness nor the exile being remembered in the Passover meal, but the escape from Egypt. Not guilt, but promise.

The escape was purchased at a horrible price. Perhaps that could be assuaged only by the beating on one's chest because freedom had been purchased so dearly and was so often not lived up to. Focusing on the sins of the exile in the traditional telling of the Passover story changes its liberating focus.

As noticed before in this account, a popular theology of Isaac's acceptance of his own sacrifice made him a "lamb for the sacrifice" figure in Jesus' day. John begins his account with "Here is the Lamb of God"—not Isaac, but Jesus. This imagery picks up on the association of Passover with forgiveness of sin.

The Passover theme is not focused on sacrifice for itself as we make it but on a call to escape to new life, a call to leave behind the past and its encumbrances and strike out for freedom. It both included and did not include a sense of redemption: being bought again is in the story, but it is a being bought back from slavery, not from personal guilt. It was not originally a sacrifice of personal redemption. The tradition would grow. By the time it is recounted in Numbers, the sacrifice of a male goat acts as the sin offering (28:22), reflecting concern about guilt in the Babylonian era. But here the sins lifted up are sins of omission rather than commission.

Remember, a study of the sacrificial system in the Bible begins with the book of Leviticus. The many sacrifices listed there—of gift and atonement, of burnt and peace offerings—are noted as sacrifices made only for sins committed in ignorance. These are the sins that we might rather call disjunctions, breaks in the human condition: the failure to keep a religious custom or a vow; perplexity with the dream state of a night's emission; the mystery of birth, its partition.

At the time, the mystery of these breaks was not understood. Something was needed to heal brokenness in the human psyche or breaches in community. These breaches were also understood as signaling something broken in the human-divine relationship: childbirth, skin eruptions, genital discharges; a broken peace in community life.

Leviticus and the biblical record are clear: these sacrifices were thought to assuage an offended deity. These sacrifices had a special burden in the Babylonian exile, but the blood was spattered against the altar, not upon oneself. We were confronting reconciliation with the whole, the community with God, rather than with personal sin. Everyone must be right with God. The psalmist and the prophets will say that God takes no delight in these sacrifices; he just desires the presentation of a repentant heart.

There is no remission for presumptuous sin in Leviticus. The letter to the Hebrews nails the coffin shut: if we willfully persist in sin after having received the knowledge of the truth, there no longer remains a sacrifice for sins (10:26–27). The writer intends to warn us. The writer of 1 John will disallow forgiveness for a mortal sin—evidently for not believing in God's Son (5:16).

That is the biblical record, but beside this biblical word, another reality pervaded. Atonement for unwitting sins in the popular mind came to be atonement for presumptuous sins by the time of Jesus' ministry. The popular belief was that Isaac's sacrifice brought redemption. But the original story was not about redemption from sin but from failing to place God above all else (sin, of course, denies that, wants sin to be about our human failings, but not about our wanting independence from God). Isaac was redeemed, but not from sin.

Leviticus, written in the time of the exile, the temple destroyed and sacrifices no longer practiced in the manner it describes, testifies to the puzzlement of the human condition and the presumption of guilt so common to our human condition—*what have I done to deserve this?*

The biblical answer for forgiveness of sin is found in the prayers of the Psalms and the preaching of the crucifixion, not the supper.

Instead of the concern with presumed guilt, Jesus' meals, lacking worry over kosher menu or guest list, show the liberty of the child of God. The supper on the night he is handed over is a summation of Jesus' restoration of creation's intention. Rather than sacrifice for sin, it asks us to explore new ways to live in the coming Passover of our day.

Betrayal happened at the meal. Betrayal is the most unacceptable offense one could deliver to someone at a meal. This is a betrayal we all fear being guilty of: "Is it I, Lord?" We fail to stay true to the unboundedness of love. We offend and betray our deepest commitments. But the meal itself is not expiation for sin; there is no slaughtered lamb on the menu (perhaps the result of a later theological elision). Jesus, host of the meal, is the slaughtered lamb. His is the blood we iconically spatter against the doorposts of our lives, not just for our personal failings, but also to make the world whole again. Against this important but rather unhappy imagery, the supper invitingly calls us to live in the new creation John shows us in his story.

Instead, we focus on sacrifice, and even then we may not get it right. Sacrificing was intended to release the power of life, not just to slay. The ancient custom is meticulously adapted to altar and temple in the book of Leviticus. The point John makes clear is that Jesus replaced the temple, and therefore there need not be any more lamb sacrifice. This fulfills of the prophets' complaint that God did not have any desire for the blood of animals.

In our covenantal relationship, we join one another in the sacrifice of praise around our tables, a new way to release the power of Christ's life into our world.

Odyssey

Almost providentially, the American film maker Ken Burns, in *Baseball*, captures the meaning of Passover with his salute to Jack Roosevelt Robinson, grandson of a slave, who on April 17, 1947, made his way to first base, becoming the first African American in the modern era to play the major leagues. It was Passover. The youngest male in a family in Brooklyn was asking the familiar question, "Why is this night different from all other nights?" The father answered, "Because a black man is playing in major league baseball" (*Christian Century*, July 15, 2008, 32).

7: Filters Through the Centuries

Originally, Jesus' humanity was uppermost in the Christian's confession. John says: "We declare to you what was from the beginning, what we have heard, what we have seen with our eyes, what we have looked at and touched with our hands, concerning the word of life" (1 John 1:1). Even as the creeds began to be formulated, early Christians fought against the Monophysites (those who believe in one nature) to keep the equal division of man and God in Jesus.

Perhaps the absence of a recitation of the events of Christ's life in the creeds is due to this carefulness. I have often argued with myself that the line "suffered under Pontius Pilate" was synecdoche, part for the whole. But God's self-revelation in the lives of the Hebrew people also is missing in the creeds. We skip from belief in God, Father almighty, creator of heaven and earth, to Jesus Christ. In both instances, the omission has the result of downplaying God's actions in the humanity of our faith, a key characteristic of the Judeo-Christian understanding.

The issue of Jesus' birth was at first important because it explained that he was a human being, and only later was Mary's virginity used to defend Jesus' godliness.

Certain overlays were placed across the understanding of the Supper, affecting its meaning. In the first century, the overlays were tradition, issues of sin and sacrifice, and the disciples' understanding of Jesus.

By the opening of the second century, only a bishop could

celebrate the Eucharist, and only approved believers could join in the sacrament. This was the practical result of their situation, but it had theological effects. As the century developed, only those who believed what the bishops taught were allowed to partake. The effect was that faith in Jesus was being valued less than faith in the bishops' teaching. The elements became holy in themselves: no longer were they "the common bread and drink of Jesus' table"; they became the bread of immortality," as Ignatius would say.

The traditional Jewish prayer of thanksgiving that Jesus had uttered at the feedings became words by which the bishops could change the elements into Jesus' body and blood. In taking the bread and wine, the believer's flesh and blood were nourished by transformation, becoming the flesh and blood of the incarnate Jesus. Paul's direction to eat and drink simply in remembrance of Jesus Christ became a means of changing the elements into the body and blood of Christ.

It is beyond the scope of this book to trace this continuing development through the many church fathers. I am in debt to Professor Charles C. Cochrane for the following summary.

The earliest Christian liturgies have no reference to eating Jesus in the Lord's Supper. The ancient Egyptian liturgy, which may be traced back to the *Didache,* has no reference to institutional words or to the body and blood of Christ. With Ignatius of Antioch (d. 117 CE), Communion became a means of uniting with Christ, the bread and medicine of immortality. The Docetists, who were declared heretics very early because they said that Christ only seemed to have a human body and did not suffer and die on the cross, also were accused of rejecting the Eucharist because they refused to admit that it is the flesh of Jesus Christ. For Ignatius, Jesus is being eaten.

Justin Martyr, in the middle of the second century, said that the bread is not common bread and the wine not common drink; rather, these are the flesh and blood of the incarnate Jesus. This is how he understood Jesus' words, "This is my body ... this is my blood." In the *Didache* of about the same time, the Eucharist was written about as a thank offering. Throughout the Christian family, there are different understandings.

The arguments rose to a fever pitch in the Arian heresy of the fourth century, as Arius attempted to make Jesus more man than God and was opposed by Augustine. But even this argument must be seen in its context. By the time of Arius, the philosophical meaning of essence had become so challenged that the equality of the human and Godhead had been lost. If God is perfect, the argument went, then God is unchanging, and the "logos," the Son, would be one step lower and not fully God.

The filter that lay across the page of understanding for Arius and Augustine was Neoplatonism, a filter most Christians do not even recognize today, though it still has its consequences. The development was complicated. In the third century, Plotinus interpreted Plato's ideas and taught that God is all perfect, matter is inferior, the self is to be denied, and salvation is a rising of the soul in a final mystic union with the divine. For most of Christian history from that time on, people just assumed that Plato was right: knowledge comes from ideas, from what we grasp by the intellect alone—not from what we sense. It has been said that nothing is more important in understanding Christian belief about the Eucharist than understanding Plato's stance on this. Essences are always more real than what we grasp. The elements could cause the hair on the nape of your neck to rise because intellectually you grant them that power.

Augustine called Arius's understanding of Jesus heretical, but he, too, held the Platonic understanding of essence. Augustine, and those who would hold his opinion, argued that Christ's being, his essence, was the same as that of the Father and that at the consecration, bread and wine became the body and blood of Christ even though its outward appearance remained that of the bread and wine on their tables. In partaking, they argued, the communicant becomes of one nature with Christ.

As the years succeeded, the argument would center on how this change in the bread and wine occurred. Was the Mass a re-sacrifice of Christ upon the cross or simply a sign of that sacrifice? Had Christ's death once and for all freed us from sin, or was the Mass a necessary application of that sacrifice, without which one could not benefit from the salvation Jesus offered? The Reformation would occur principally over this methodological argument. The continuing issue of essence would remain much the same for the Reformers, particularly for Luther and, though not as clearly recognized, other Protestants.

Huldrych Zwingli, alone among the Reformers, insisted that it was *belief* in the once-and-for-all sacrifice of Jesus, through the gift of the Holy Spirit, which was the means of grace, not the sacrament. The sacrament could not free the conscience; only God could do that. The sacrament could not cleanse, create, or strengthen faith. According to Zwingli, the sacraments are signs by which one says to the church that one's aim is to be Christ's follower. "No one comes to Christ unless the Father draws him." The Supper does not give faith, for faith must be present before we come. This faith is not in the elements but in God's acts.

To this day, there is a divide, with the greater part of the church choosing to elevate the nature of the elements. Even the Protestant wing—to which I belong—subtly, if not apologetically, bows to the nature side of the argument. The rarity and heaviness of its celebrations are evidence. In these more recent years the theorizing about what taking the sacrament can "do" for you—remitting your sin, perfecting your character—makes the sacrament an issue of essence rather than action. And so we search for the manger and fail to experience the incarnation found in living out the Supper.

Here, then, are the traces that answer our earlier question: what happened? The church turned from a call to openness to the sensibility of safety. Christians saw what had happened to their forebears. They had been cut off from their land, their patrimony, and their authority. The church needed to protect itself. Theologically, Jesus' birth stories strengthened the church. However, when believers felt threatened, the stories of his life lost the power to make them open and accepting.

Furthermore, it was much easier to return to the old ways of the sacrificial system than to turn to the freedom of the creation, the new creation, as the good news according to John had called them to do. In our experience, we allow the table to have boundaries too, and not just with regard to those welcomed to it. We fence the table by thinking that Communion deals only with salvation from our sins rather than the unbounded freedom of living for others. Salvation from sins no doubt accounts for the fencing of the altar, the iconostasis, which has proved sturdier than the filigreed latticework fencing the altars of European cathedrals.

Christians have added other filigrees to their practical faith experience, hunted here and there, to buttress the church and their faith. Some are not overlays as on a page; rather these overlays, these powerful filigrees, are their testimonies that communing may improve your character and wash away your sins.

Certain figures in history have had unbelievable influence on the people who live after them and on their course of thinking. We immediately think of Jesus Christ as one such person. Joan of Arc inspires noble dissent. Saint Augustine was another. His influence on Western thought still affects our intellectual world and shapes the thinking in our churches. Interestingly enough, we are affected by how he arrived at what he believed as much as by his belief itself. His obsession with guilt still shapes our spiritual lives and the way we approach Holy Communion. We take the sacrament with heaviness because his view was that Jesus died to take away our sin and guilt.

Augustine was not baptized as an infant. The custom of his day (354–430 CE) was still adult baptism. Though his mother, Monica, prayed and worked for his conversion, it did not happen while he was young. Instead, Augustine lived with one mistress or another from the age of seventeen to thirty-two and raised hell around town with a wild group of guys. Then he was famously converted at age thirty-two. Hearing a voice call him to take up and read the Scriptures, he began to prepare himself for baptism, making his confession of faith at the age of thirty-three.

His life experience in turn influenced our understanding of Communion. One way to look at Augustine's writings is that for the rest of his life, he repented his youthful passion. His great themes became human sinfulness and the grace of God. Only God could reach down and lift a fallen sinner like him, he felt. Because of his great revulsion for his past, he saw our physical nature as suspect, just like the world itself. According to Augustine, that which is important is the inner and the moral. He felt called to reflect on his desperate sinning and how gracious God had been to save him. This sense of the guilt of original sin came to pervade Western Christianity.

We have a window into his argument on original sin in his controversy with Pelagius. Born the same year as Augustine, Pelagius was dead twelve years before Augustine died. From in the British Isles, Pelagius settled in Rome about 400 CE. One is tempted to wonder whether the milieu of his birth (the cold of the North) affected his thinking as Augustine's (a lush north Africa) may have affected his. In any case, Pelagius held to the freedom of the will, believing that if he were meant to do so, he could overcome sin. He did not espouse a belief in original sin, which Augustine believed unalterably prevents human freedom. Augustine believed he had been saved from sins he could never have overcome himself. Grace, he taught, infuses the love in us that gradually transforms our characters. But to Pelagius, baptism conveys the grace of remission of sins and is our mark of forgiveness.

The end of the story for Pelagius was that he was named a heretic. The triumph of Augustine's position was that children must be baptized for the remission of original sin and that sinlessness is impossible in this life. We can concur with this latter judgment, but why did the charge of heresy arise? Underneath the argument about grace and original sin is a deeper worry. It appeared to Augustine that Pelagius's position meant that we could save ourselves by thinking and doing. If so, where was the need for a savior? We could work out our own salvation … so, then, what would the sacrament mean?

I must give Augustine this: as I have sometimes stood in wonder viewing the great cathedrals of Europe, the Rockefeller churches and chapels in this country, I have asked myself would all this grandeur, this beauty, these organs with their manifold pipes, ever have come about without him, without the driving force of guilt, of needing to make up for our sins? Would the glory and wonder of creation have sufficed? The effect of Augustine's concentration on guilt and sin became the hallmark of Western Christianity in stone and psychology. It need not be assumed that this judgment is fully correct. Cathedrals also speak to God's magnificent greatness.

Let us turn to the subject of mystery.

Odyssey

Consider the modernity of this history: a song by Bob Dylan. Test your feelings, not just your thinking. Maybe you will be just curious enough to wonder why a folk singer sang of Saint Augustine in the sixties. In the seventies I heard Dylan sing "I Dreamed I Saw St. Augustine,"

> I dreamed I saw St. Augustine alive as you or me, tearing through these quarters in the utmost misery: with a blanket underneath his arm and a coat of solid gold, searching for the very souls who already have been sold.

> Arise, arise, he cried so loud in a voice without restraint; come out ye gifted kings and queens and hear my sad complaint.
> No martyr is among ye now who you can call your own.

> But go on your way accordingly and know you're not alone.
> I dreamed I saw St. Augustine alive with fiery breath, and I dreamed I was amongst the ones that put him out to death.

> Oh, I awoke in anger so alone and terrified;
> I put my fingers against the glass and bowed
> My head and cried.

Dylan cries against our present age with its easy sloughing off of guilt, its easy dismissal of the consequences of our actions. His sorrow is poignant and arresting; it is arresting to have Augustine invoked in such a secular medium and at the height of the 1960s, an era obsessed with personal freedom.

We take Communion, and Dylan tells us that a very alive Augustine rends his clothes and mourns and that he and we, by extension, are the ones who have put him out to death. And we feel it, thinking perhaps that taking Communion deals only with salvation from sin instead of living for others, that it deals only with the vertical relationship with God, the mystery, and the hair on the napes of our necks rising upon communing.

8: WHAT ABOUT MYSTERY?

Jeffrey Hawthorne says in one of his hymns, "Lord, you make the common holy." Let's consider that.

One difficulty with the approach I am suggesting to Holy Communion is that it will be felt to lack the sense of the mystery we have traditionally associated with the sacrament. We have not yet fully dealt with Vicar Keach's observation about hair rising on the nape of the neck. Roman Catholic observance and surely the Orthodox Church's experience celebrate mystery. Our ambivalence about the possibility of a daily sacrament asks us to look a little deeper.

Our meals do not always, or even usually, lend themselves to being "sacraments" of some deeper meaning. Wonder bread is hardly manna (though as a staple of my childhood, I loved it and still remember its cottony taste) or the life and death of Jesus to us. It does not measure up to what we have come to think of as sacrament. In our harried time, we entertain less and do not often experience a sense of open community. The dining room table is hardly a communal altar. It may be piled high with books or mail as we hurry in and out.

Sometimes, meal times are a family's worst experience of community or greater meaning. If a family meal time still persists— and this is not often a regular occurrence in this era—a parent's attempt to mention world or national events or ask what deeper meaning has been experienced in a day's schedule may draw only a "huh?" from the kids. I once asked one of my sons for one of his worst mealtime memories, and he said it was having to say something he appreciated about the person next to him, usually a brother, at Thanksgiving. I had tried to use this tack as a form of grace before the meal without much success.

From a child's ready "yuck" over the beets to a spouse's polite reservation over a new recipe, an uncomfortable silence or outright rebellion may sometimes more likely characterize the meal than a ritual blessing. Our true ritual words are "at least take two bites," though we may have said, "Bless us, O Lord, for these thy gifts we are about to receive through the mercy of Jesus Christ our Lord."

The closest we may come to experiencing a deeper reality, reminding us of past occasions or stirring our thanksgiving, may be sharing pizza or being served what we have come to call comfort food. But even on these occasions, it is doubtful that we have learned to name the experience as sacramental—especially if one of the kids yells, "I hate pepperoni!"

Nevertheless, to listen to Jesus' good news is to find that joining in a meal with others means anticipating and entering the coming of God's kingdom. As I have said before, Jesus begins his ministry with eating. He denied that meals should be open only to friends, because for him meals were about joining Abraham, Isaac, and Jacob in eating in the kingdom of God, where everyone was welcome from east and west, north and south, downtown, or out in the hedgerows. He insists that we invite the folks who can't return the invitation!

Despite our on-the-run meals, we know the mystery of this down deep. When we tell a host or hostess that the meal was heavenly or that the crème brûlée was divine, it is more than polite chatter. Consider the run of movies lately that feast our eyes on the preparation and eating of marvelous food: *Babette's Feast, Mostly Martha, Like Water for Chocolate,* and many more. Deep down, we also know feasting when we are satisfied with crackers, sardines, good conversation, and good memories.

Some would like to think that God's ultimate revelation comes through intense Bible study or being caught up in rapturous church music or even some heightening or deprivation of the senses. For Jesus, God is revealed in the anticipation and fellowship that comes in simple eating. No wonder he was so upset over the rules that had come to bind meals' being shared with others, rules that said you had to eat only with your own kind. "Ho, everyone who thirsts," had become severely dehydrated.

In thinking of the mystery of sacrament, we will have to redefine our meanings.

In this chapter, then, we bring together a number of threads: the meaning of *sacrament,* an early church term for mystery; the meaning of mystery and our need for it in life; and some reflection on the particular sense of overwhelming awe that my approach may seem to lack. And then we will address the following question: is Holy Communion the sacrament, the sign, or the implementation of a deeper mystery?

The early Roman church used the word sacrament to translate the word "mystery." The Greek mystery religions had used it for their rites of initiation. The term "sacrament" had the legal connotation of making a commitment or taking an oath. The Anabaptists had some problems with the term since they did not believe in taking oaths. Some preferred the word "ceremonies," but they wanted to keep the element of commitment that *sacramentum* had. Others preferred "ordinances," such as the Baptist tradition, perhaps to steer away from Catholicism while keeping a sense of order.

Still, for Anabaptists like Marpeck, the Lord's Supper and baptism were witnesses of a deeper reality. While some of the Anabaptists wanted to avoid giving the Supper's elements a reality of a bodily or corporeal presence, the idea that these rites were *witnesses* permitted them great depth. Consider the fact that *witness* is the same New Testament word as *martyr,* a dying for the faith, and you see the important overtones.

It was to witness to these deeper relationships that Jesus' ministry was so much about eating. He used a welcoming gesture in one homely act to recall an ancient history stretching back before Abraham to ancient Middle Eastern tradition in order to point forward to the open acceptance everyone would find at the celestial banquet in God's eternal day. He did this without words, or what would later become known as rubrics, to define how one is to celebrate a rite. This was such a phenomenal difference in the stratified society of his religious world that it shook the invitees, the hosts, the religious observers, and his new followers to the core. Eat with sinners? With zealots? With the non-kosher? His witness would bring his death, his martyrdom, because it upset the status quo, an upset Rome could not have in its understanding of pax.

Notice, I call it phenomenal, a phenomenon. Without Jesus preaching about what he was doing, the people understood. No words to explain or organize his actions were needed. And because the inclusive meals so touched them all, they were deeply religious experiences. The social fabric of their day was being torn. The categories of their religious life as to who was holy, separate, and who was not, who was in and who was out, were turned on their heads. Their whole understanding of the meaning and rules of purity was rewritten. Kosher no longer referred only to specific foods blessed by a rabbi or to meals with one's friends only; kosher meant celebrating community.

Part of our difficulty with missing the everyday wonder of our lives is that we have misunderstood the term *religious*. We think of it primarily in churchy, Godward, or eerie terms. A more encompassing definition of the religious experience is having your worldview challenged, maybe torn or turned upside down; it means re-evaluating fundamental views toward life when things are turned upside down. September 11, 2001, was certainly a religious experience in every sense of that word for Americans.

To think of meals as revelatory, as religious, challenged the disciples' worldview. It challenges ours, too. It is not just eating wonderful fruit from the garden that is religious, but its preparation, its reminder of sacrifice, and its welcoming enjoyment. It is all of this and more.

What Jesus was demonstrating was the essential core, the nature of what would later be named a sacrament. God is as welcoming and inviting as a good meal. Against an exclusive view of God, a judging

God, this view that God is welcoming has yet to win the day in the gut understandings of many who consider themselves religious. How can it be as simple as sitting down to dinner with another?

For a meal to be a sacrament, one need not remark that Mom or Dad has worked hard to put food on the table (that is, sacrificed); that someone has taken thought to make an attractive setting and presentation of a meal; or to recall that a chicken has been killed for our sustenance and enjoyment. These are the unsaid realities, occasionally remarked but often forgotten or tacitly accepted, which make a meal more than just a way to sate our hunger.

How then did that last meal Jesus took with his disciples become misunderstood? You only have to look at the arguments at the time of the Reformation to see the long arc of development. Argument upon argument was piled up over what was meant exactly by Jesus' words, "This is my body; this is my blood. Do this in remembrance of me." What was the meaning of *this*? What is a *remembrance*? *Body? Blood?* Wasn't Jesus saying, 'I want to be your food, I want to share what I am with you, my neighbor, and everyone? By saying he wants to be our food, Jesus was not suggesting he would be literally eaten, but that all he was and is and did was and is for our sustenance.

Jesus was not telling the disciples to do something new. They were always eating. So as they ate, Jesus was reminding them to think of it in sacramental terms. At that final fellowship meal, he was not giving a ritual direction in saying these words. He was summing up his entire ministry and life with them, saying, "Eating together in a covenant of love is what I have been about, accepting you as you are, even the one who will betray me tonight and the one who will deny me tonight."

John most clearly picks up his meaning. "If you want to share in my life," says Jesus, "be part of my will for the world; know me as I have known my Father. Then as you eat your meals together, think of me. It will bring remembrance of me. It will also help you think of what is wrong in your life that has kept you from community. This will be redemptive."

And true enough, in the light of the resurrection, they knew him in the breaking of bread at Emmaus and on a Sunday evening when he appeared to them behind locked doors and asked if they had anything to eat. They knew him in sharing a breakfast of fish beside the shore of Lake Tiberias, and during the forty days before he ascended, we are told in Acts 1:4, he ate with them. (Actually, you have to catch that in a footnote, since most translations say he was staying with them.) Eating with them was what Jesus had been about. They would not need rubrics to hallow the meals they shared together. Can you imagine what those meals must have been like, the learning that took place?

When they retold the stories of the feeding of the thousands, they formed them as occasions of thanksgiving, Eucharist.

But you have to understand these Reformation arguments about the *this* and the *do* in light of fifteen hundred years of history: years of craning one's neck to see the lifted host amid the ever increasing panoply of miters and vestments and processionals; years of confessing one's unworthiness to take the sacrament; years of seeing only the priest commune; and years of failing to understand that the institutional words themselves came late to the rubrics of the Mass. You have to remember that only with the Middle Ages did the kneeling before the raised host begin. Only in the Middle Ages was feeling and personal angst—perhaps engendered by war and pestilence—about the sacrament introduced.

The words we now call institutional words were not included in the home meals and agapes of the second century so that there would be no confusion over their meaning. It is true that in the early teens of the second century, a priest or bishop was already being required to host at the agape. That gives more than a hint that the bread and cup (not always wine, if a family could only afford water) were being held in a different kind of esteem from in the Lord's day, but theologically, this had not yet become dogma. Dogma came later out of experience, true enough, but that does not mean one cannot return to the original intention.

The rubrics, the lifting of the host, the vestments, the reservation of the chalice, and the replacement of a parent with a priest at the meal had all come about accidentally. In part the changes came naturally—believers wanted to keep the old ways while asking,

"How do we properly glorify Jesus?" These arguments still surface in our newspapers about proper dress at church. But for the early church, these actions had arisen out of believers' grief over the loss of their master and the assumption that it must be their fault that he had neither returned nor helped them overcome their tribulations. They felt they needed atonement in the sacrifice of the Mass. The actions arose out of a misunderstanding that it was not *what* they were eating, but it was the *action* of their eating together that Jesus had been concerned with.

So it would come about that priests would speak of saying the Mass, getting the words right, but they would be performing the Eucharist, acting. This distinction was too easily lost. And the fact is that from the seventh to the nineteenth century in most churches, only the priests communed; the congregation watched. Believers' distance from the host deeply informed their thinking about mystery.

It is the observation of Walter Klaassen that the Anabaptists saw the holy in the everyday. For them, he says,

> there were no holy words. The words from the New Testament institute the supper but do not consecrate it: "This is my body," does not change the bread. Nor are there holy things. The bread remains bread and ordinary bread should be used and be treated as ordinary bread. And, there is no holy place. The supper may be celebrated anywhere. There is no holy person, a server may be chosen from out of the congregation. Finally, there is no holy time. The communion need not be observed on Sundays only, or on special days. (page 11)

Andrew M. Greeley, priest, sociologist, and novelist, says that liturgy—we could say sacramental meaning—ought to arise out of the experiences of grace in the secular world. He makes two assumptions:

1. That the self-communication of God (experiences of hope, renewal, sacraments of grace, the dance of the Spirit,

whatever name one wants to use) occurs not only ... and not primarily in interludes of worship, but also ... and especially in the grace-full persons, events and objects of daily life.

2. Among the purposes of Sacramental Experience in the liturgy is a "correlation" of the experiences of God's self-communication in secular life with the overarching experiences of the religious Tradition, so that each correlate may illumine the other. The goal of the Sacraments is to rearticulate, refine, recollect, and re-present secular sacraments and thus to deepen and enrich and challenge them by integrating them into the Community and the Tradition.

To illustrate these assumptions, Greeley cites the love, joy, pride, and good wishes that parents bring to the baptism of a child and the graceful descriptions of a bride and groom's love for each other that are lifted up in toasts at a wedding banquet. Perhaps, he says, these good wishes ought rather to come before the homily of the wedding service. Drawing on these observations, the homily then can be a response to the grace already present, the communication of God that has already occurred in parents and lovers:

Life, love, renewal—the most elementary experiences of human life—are the sacramental experiences that correlate with the Sacraments. They merge in the Eucharist as a correlate of the experience of community through which humans find their life, exercise their love and experience their renewal. *The Eucharist is not the central sacrament because God or church arbitrarily determined that it be so, but because community is the central experience of the human condition; the common meal is the most normal and ordinary method of celebrating life and love and renewal in community. In our day, the family meals at Christmas and Thanksgiving, interludes that purport to be—and often are—celebrations of life and love and renewal are superb correlates of the heavenly banquet ... Eucharist, even when mumbled quietly in Latin or a bit more loudly in English, had and has great power over the faithful precisely because they perceive, perhaps only pre-consciously, that it is a time of the coming together of the secular and the religious, of meals and The Meal, of our banquets on earth and the Banquet in God's kingdom.* (Greeley, *America* 379–383, 390, emphasis added)

In a bind, we have confused panoply with the amelioration of guilt and the tinkling of a bell or the solemnity of a ritual with mystery and wonder. We miss the wonder of daily life that we know so well—seeing sunrise and sunset, the birth of a baby, the forgiveness of a spouse or friend whom we have offended, or the taste of freshly baked bread or crisp vegetables or the sweet fruit of the vine. We know the wonder of orgasm but have been so negatively and perversely conditioned by society and the church that we miss the sacrament it opens us to. It is perhaps the time we most often name the deity. Missing the depths in life, we have missed the mystery.

Jesus had a word for us. When talking with his questioners about the temple, he told them, "Something greater than the temple is here." So caught up with the glory of a great building, they had missed the something greater; they had missed Jesus. They had missed the sacred. We too can miss the something greater if we are more concerned with holy days and holy ways, more concerned with the bread and the wine, than with the presence of the One gathered with the two or three of us.

I once heard Reuel Howe, who had a long ministry in helping people become more human, more loving, and fully Christian, say that we must learn to live so that we can look for the eternal Thou in each other; but we still must know that we live in the It, the world of everyday functions. What Howe is asking of us is to look for the significance, the "something greater" in others and our experience; to be in awe of the universe or the mystery of another person. What do we hold sacred? The wonder of our world? The mystery of another person? Mystery is there without institutional words. Of course, we know how difficult it is to live such mystery. Perhaps that intensifies the mystery.

So, we come to the question asked earlier. Is Holy Communion the sacrament or sign—or, better, the implementation—of a deeper mystery?

Holy Communion is the sign and implementation of the community we find in the church. Because our era devalues the corporate experience and the body-of-Christ image of the church, we look for mystery in more individualistic terms of spirituality and feeling and miss the wonder of the new creation to which we are called. Because our understanding and appreciation of community in our era is skewed and even broken, we find it difficult to appreciate this understanding of Communion. It is easier to keep it privatized and devoted to making us whole, covering our sins, than confessing our failure to be the body of Christ in our world.

Because the Supper is a corporate meal and not the private transaction we make it, eating bread and drinking wine becomes an act of contrition for our forgiveness rather than celebrating our being raised into new life. Also because the Supper is a corporate meal, our children and others need to be partaking with us for it to have its fullest understanding. This is also a mystery.

Paul lifts up this mystery when he talks with the Corinthians about the meaning of the Supper. In order to rein in the practices of overeating and of not sharing, Paul reminds his people that the Supper had a dimension they were missing. In taking the cup of blessing and partaking of the bread, they were entering a mystical communion, a koinonia, which was something more, something different from a neighborhood potluck. The one loaf had a symbolic meaning of uniting them as one in Christ, making them one in him.

Discerning the body meant discerning this relationship. It did not mean understanding the bread as the symbol of what Jesus did for your sins. Time and again, people who do not want to admit children or unbelievers to the table misunderstand this. "Children are not old enough," they say. "The unbelieving guest cannot understand it." Scripture denies all of that. Children were eager participants in the Passover meal because they knew they were part of the body on its way to a greater future. Guests have always been intrigued by Passover meals, "See how they love one another."

Earlier in his letter to the Corinthians, Paul places these meal times in the context of the old covenant's sacrifice, where a covenant is made, and also in the context of taking care not to eat what had been sacrificed to idols because of the danger of suggesting that you were "at one" with the purposes of the idol's cult. By negative example, he shows them the bonds that develop when people eat together.

All of this has great significance for our worship today. We complain about the loss of mystery, although we could be greatly helped by applying Paul's principles. Beginning a service of worship with the ancient words, or a creative adaptation, of the sursum corda, "The Lord be with you," and its response, "And also with you," would strike a note of the mystery that we seek. Our meeting is more than, "Hi. Good morning!" It is, after all, Jesus' greeting during his resurrection appearances, reminding us that he is again with us—"Where two or three are gathered, there am I in the midst." "Lift up your hearts" is a call to turn from wandering thoughts and place our earthly cares in the care of God. We tend not to think this way today.

Paul's warnings to the Corinthian Christians about the fellowship surrounding meat dedicated to idols are appropriate for our day. Who worries about where the butcher has gotten our steak? But the environmental destruction of feedlots and the danger of fats to our health may make us take care. Considering that marbled steaks may signify a salute to the good life, there could be certain idolatries at stake. Why do we have a need to eat high on the steer? Does that question even register in our thinking?

But the point is that our fellowship together has to have different values than may be present in our other community fellowships. Some of these—service clubs, Masons—may be more benign than political alliances, but the issue for Paul would be whether these groups ask an allegiance of us that is counter to the allegiance we owe to God. The other issue would be whether the time we are willing to give these other groups overshadows the time we invest in the body of Christ. What is the meaning of koinonia to us, and how is its mystery made real in our daily lives? If someone suffers because of the way we live, what is our response? When we begin to worship, so we recall the suffering in Africa?

We are not always aware of the occasions and nature of mystery in our lives today. There are those who, the hair raising on the nape of the neck, experience the supper more mysteriously. In 1981 I was enrolled in a Clinical Pastoral Education seminar at St. Elisabeths Hospital in Washington, D.C., then caring for the man who had attempted to assassinate President Reagan. In those months Holy Communion was taken every morning according to the Episcopal rite: no homily (sans Calvin), the Scriptures of the day, the passing of the peace, prayers and communion as we stood in a circle around the table. For the first time in my life, I heard a fellow pastor say that she could not live, could not function through the day, if she did not first take the sacrament; it was life itself. Her words brought me to a new step on the journey. But mystery is not necessarily only signified by the tinkling bell of the Roman Mass or the hidden actions behind the iconostasis. To paraphrase a secular song, "Love Is Where You Find It," by Earl K. Brent and Nacio Herb Brown,

Mystery is where you find it ...
don't be blinded ... it's everywhere ...

Odyssey

A poem

Jesus is here!
O could my eyes
Tear apart the veiling skies,
What joyous start
would wake my heart,
My glorious Lord!

Lord, thou art here!
My heart sees thee!
Knows that thou see-
est even me!
I am forgiven, accepted, loved
by thee, my Lord.
                    —Winifred Waltner

I first heard Mrs. Waltner read her poem at a meditation she gave in Jerusalem in 1992. I realized how Christ's presence is real to us in many ways. Is it more real in the Communion service?

9: WE PREACH CHRIST CRUCIFIED

Lift high the cross, the love of Christ proclaim
till all the world adore his sacred name.

—George W. Kitchin

In a fine treatise on the subject of sacrifice, *Saved from Sacrifice: A Theology of the Cross,* S. Mark Heim, who teaches at Andover Newton Theological School, says we may learn from the classic explanations of the atonement, but we must also learn from Rene Girard's refutation of sacred violence and assertion that rising from the baptismal waters is to live without scapegoating, to live forward rather than backward, as it were. Is it only a divine act whereby we are transformed? Can it be both? In a prequel to his book, Heim says:

> Protestants historically take their stand on the confession that they can be reconciled with God because of the sacrifice of Christ: "We preach Christ, and him crucified." Roman Catholics point to the same event as the sacramental center of Christian life, with the words from the Gospel of John, "the Lamb of God, who takes away the sins of the world." Eastern Orthodox position the significance of the death in relation to the resurrection, proclaiming in the Easter liturgy

that "Christ has risen from the dead, by death trampling upon death and bringing life to those in the tomb." The Gospels, the heart of Christian Scripture, are in large measure passion narratives. The central Christian liturgical act, the celebration of the Lord's Supper, points insistently to the death. The peak of the Christian year, at Good Friday and Easter, revolves around it. (Heim, *Christian Century, 3/7/01, p.* 12)

I would agree with Professor Heim, but I would take a different tack. It is an accident of religious history that "the central Christian liturgical act, the celebration of the Lord's Supper, points insistently to the death." This was not Jesus' original intent. His death, while forced upon him by Rome, was of his own free choice. In that choice, we are to live. His meal was a paradigm for how we are to live. To speak of Christ's sacrifice is to use the language of the church, not Jesus. That is the point I have been making throughout.

The different tack is this: we *preach* Christ crucified. In the Supper, we celebrate his life. We know death to be part of life but not life's insistent focus. This is particularly important since we know that it is liturgy that has imported suffering and death and forgiveness ("broken for you") into the Last Supper, not Jesus. The words, "broken for you," are not in the original. Even the phrase "for the remission of sins" was added later—only in Matthew—and speaks to, as we have seen, the growing issues over atonement in the young church. To focus solely on the death is to commit the Communion service to guilt, heaviness, and regret.

To focus solely on the death is to ignore Jesus' life. Professor Heim said here, "Christian faith is as unimaginable without Jesus' life (his actions and teaching) as without his death." The sad truth of the matter is that historically, that has not been believers' experience in the Communion service. Even in the liturgy of worship, one has only to cite the Apostles' Creed to note how Jesus' life has been collapsed into "suffered under Pontius Pilate" as synecdoche for his whole life, obligingly placing the onus on Rome rather than "the Jews." If the church had understood and preached this, it could have saved us from the worst of anti-Semitism, the pogroms and Holocaust.

The Nicene Creed says no more, and only in the year 2003 was a decade added to the rosary referring to events of Jesus' life—and these are ritual events like the dedication in the temple and his baptism, not his welcoming program of eating meals with friend and foe or his conflict with temple authorities and the law or his encounter with a Syrophoenecian woman and his learning from it.

It is true that the Gospels are in large measure passion narratives. Before Peter's confession, Mark's thematic concern is to show that Jesus was the Christ. From the confession onward, it was Mark's intention to show that it was necessary for the Christ to suffer. This literary concern may have colored his account of the Last Supper to connect it with sacrifice.

It does not follow that because Mark imported the sacrifice of Christ into the meaning of the Lord's Supper, that that is what Jesus intended. Mark did so because of what was happening to Christians spiritually at the time he was writing; believers were appropriating the first covenant's sacrificial understandings. As we have seen, the popular theological understanding of the day had united Isaac's sacrifice with the Passover. But Jesus' intention in that hurried Last Supper was to invite the disciples on a new Passover journey with him. It was an invitation to live a life in the kingdom of God he had taught and lived before them.

The heaviness and sorrow in and after that Supper was because of betrayal and parting. To this the young church added Jesus' own struggle with his death.

One cannot pass over the life issues Jesus was confronting as he set his face toward Jerusalem. He was not in verbal confrontation with Rome, except for calling Herod a fox, nor did he verbally confront the absentee landowners for creating extraordinary debt. But his message was contrary to their interests and would bring his death. Why in two thousand years of church history have we ignored this? Religiously, it has something to do with construing the story of salvation as only a matter of our personal relationship with God and a denial of our complicity. Politically, it has to do with the way we become enamored of the ruling and landlord caste.

Jesus confronted his religious contemporaries' narrow understandings of religious law, particularly the everyday challenge of eating with persons not of one's kosher group: sinners, farmers, tax collectors, zealots, Pharisees, women, and persons with skin eruptions or genital discharges. The challenge was whether to walk through Samaria or not; whether to let a woman touch you or not. These were conditions so far from our experience that we can hardly fathom them. Each challenge Jesus met and opened himself to. He was open to life in all its affirmations and open to God's welcoming table.

Making these challenges to religious understandings upset the religious life of Palestine, and Rome could not have it, could not separate religious disagreement from political troublemaking. Today we see anew how religious understandings and political commitments impinge on one another. We tend to dismiss this as we read the gospel account.

To return to our argument of whether the table is the center of our worship, we concur that it is the central symbol of the great welcoming, but we have Jesus' own words for making *preaching*, rather than the Supper, the carrier of salvation. He tells Nicodemus that just as Moses lifted up the serpent in the wilderness, so must the Son of Man be lifted up, that whoever believes in him may have eternal life (John 3:14–15). This references the forgiveness brought in the wilderness when Moses lifted up a brass serpent on a pole that, when the people who had been bitten by poisonous serpents looked at it, healed people and ensured they did not die yet. We, too, look to the cross with Jesus upon it, and we are healed.

Here, in a few words, is Jesus' resolution of the atonement controversy of his and our day. As the Son of Man is lifted up, we believe in him, and believing, we have eternal life. Surely, this was Paul's message to the Philippian jailer. There is nothing here of a payment of debt. God reconciles the world and us to himself through Christ, as Paul says, not counting our trespasses against us (2 Corinthians 5:18–19).

Where the sacrificial system had been for the resolution of unintentional sins so that worshipers could approach—sins, we might say, of omission—Jesus spoke to sins of commission. This resonates with the story of the fall and the reason why the Passover and escape from Egypt probably became merged with the sacrifice system in the early church, just as was happening in popular Jewish belief in Jesus' day. John's theology of "lifting up" lifts up God's glorifying of Jesus, both his exaltation and his suffering. He was willing to die for his message of God's welcome and became like the lamb before his slaughterers, dumb. Ironically, the authorities are the ones who physically lift him up.

In our war-torn world, there is compelling reason in both our preaching of Christ crucified and in our celebrating of his life to avoid blessing violence. Some critics think the crucifixion blesses violence. Our culture has a belief that violence is regenerative, that one must die for many, that killing Saddam Hussein is better than finding peaceful ways to deal with his terrorism. Unfortunately, the American church has not preached the wisdom of the turned cheek. Indeed, much of the church accepts violence as God's way. The repetition of "God bless America" is allowed to be a benediction on violence because the church does not forthrightly engage in the media to contradict it and disassociate itself from unholy views of God. When a modern Jeremiah disputes a "God bless America" theology, all hell breaks loose. Why couldn't the church have said no to war?

"God was in Christ reconciling the world" is not testimony to God's placing Jesus on the tree, in the fashion of Abraham's attempted sacrifice of Isaac, but that God suffered with Jesus in the death dealt him by those who could not bear his message of love. We preach Christ crucified, but not by the hand of God.

In preaching, one may clarify why violence must be avoided. The Supper, on the other hand, when celebrated only in the passion mode, appears to make violence the sine qua non of the salvation story.

There is a spiritual and a logical connection between the themes of the death that arise in the celebration of the Supper. We do not advocate that all is sunshine and light as some approaches do. I have referred to the unspoken recognition that a meal has required sacrifice on the part of the one who prepares it and in terms of what is consumed. Sacrifice is a given at the heart of things. John shows it most clearly in the humbling act of feet washing at the last supper, and in doing so, he gives us a picture of another approach to death and the repudiation of love that sometimes results. A full-orbed Communion service will include life and death. It does not require that the Old Testament sacrificial system bind it to issues of atonement. Our problem is that in the years of theological development, sacrifice has acquired the barnacles of bitter questions: to whom did God pay remuneration? The Devil? That gives mighty power to the Devil.

What has happened in our celebration of Lent and its preaching is an emphasis on atonement for sins, culminating in the Maundy Thursday service. We have a need to suffer with Jesus on Good Friday for the myriad ways we are complicit in the betrayal of God's love.

Our testimony is rather this: we preach Christ crucified because his invitation to a life of love was too much for his world system to bear. He confronted his religious world with the contradiction found in their refusal to eat openly and widely with one another. They were denying their deepest truth, known to them from their father Abraham. Eating together is covenanting in peace. Instead they had chosen a life of kosher rules and kosher friendships with its consequence of excluding others.

They had chosen a kind of death. They were not honoring God in one another, especially in the least of their acquaintances. Jesus specifically rebuked their practices of inviting only those who could return an invitation and their practice of giving seating privilege according to certain honors, a practice embraced by their surrounding culture. They had settled for the pottage of a spurious birthright religion, and in the words of the writer to the Hebrews, accepting such pottage is an act that makes one to be profane (12:16).

Profanity in our day is taking the Lord's name in vain. Some even confuse profanity with scatological reference to bodily functions. To be profane, says the letter to the Hebrews, is to be irreligious: selling your birthright for a bowl of soup.

The religious leaders of Jesus' day put their understanding of God in a box, though they would not have thought of it that way, and because of that, Jesus' reproof was a threat. They thought they were the purveyors of what God wanted in the world and that Jesus was upsetting God's directives. And so, they conspired to put him to death. They understood that God had called them to a life of purity. That Jesus would eat openly with the non-kosher and programmatically send his disciples out on tours demanding a non-kosher lifestyle in their mission engagements was too much for the religious leaders to bear.

The fact was that the religious authorities were impotent to bring Jesus to heel. Religious arguments were non-starters for Rome. However, these arguments could spark Rome's interest in a preacher who was proposing that Rome's system of violence should yield to love. "Walk a second mile" and "turn the other cheek" were incendiary pieces of advice in an occupied country, precisely because their wisdom was rooted in Rome's law. Soldiers were not to require these obligations and would be court-martialed for getting caught in the Jesus trap.

Many today wish that the Palestinians could heed Jesus' advice against the occupiers of their country. "Turn the other cheek; walk the second mile." But before we point the finger at Palestinians, many of us know how impractical it seems to press Jesus' advice on the leaders of our own country, how contrary to our own history. The "divine right" of the terror in the westward expansion of our country, our acquisition of territories, should make us hesitant in offering Palestinians and Israelis counsel. Jesus was challenging his world system, religious and political, and for this he was crucified.

Now this becomes *preaching Christ crucified* when we turn to the observation of our own practices. So often we fail to do that. That is the real purpose of the Gospels. What about *our* kosher arrangements? We eat and fellowship almost totally with friends and fellow believers. What about *our* complicity with Rome? In the best of our historical responses, the church has understood this gospel, or good news, to position us over the state or the ruling philosophy of the day. So it was with Niemoller against Germany or Barth against the religious protectorate of liberal Christianity. But if we are honest, we have to struggle with the religious hegemony we want for ourselves and the theological views we have of ourselves, drawn down these two thousand years. We, too, keep kosher rules and kosher friendships personally, ecclesiastically, and politically. We, too, are afraid to reach out in love.

The preaching of the gospel of crucifixion does not have to be omitted from the Communion service. It is fitting to remember that covenanting to love others is to risk death. We know it in our home and professional lives: love isn't always understood. Washing feet may not make you CEO. Numberless stories from the integration and anti-war movements bear out how love is misunderstood. So death is part of the Communion liturgy, but that does not mean that the Communion service can only be formulated in terms of the sacrifice/guilt motif. As a meal in the time of Passover, it is a reminder to develop all of the themes of our call to freedom.

Yes, Passover themes involve sacrificial blood, including the death of the firstborn and the blood on the lintel. But a broader view emphasizes getting rid of the old, grieving its passing, and getting on with the call to freedom. Without this balance, Passover becomes mired in personal sin rather than a call to leave Egypt for the Promised Land.

In a gospel tradition that does not have a weekly-celebrated Communion, we preach the gospel of crucifixion and give our assent in the hymns we sing, as in this one from 1707:

> Alas, and did my Savior bleed?
> And did my sovereign die?
> Would he devote that sacred head for
> such a worm as I? (Watts)

In the 1885, perhaps unhappy with being called a worm, Ralph E. Hudson amended the verse this way:

At the cross, at the cross where I first
saw the light
And the burden of my heart rolled
away,
It was there by faith I received my sight,
And now I am happy all the day.

I doubt that Watts would agree to being happy all the day. Perhaps we are not, either.

We do not like to be described as worms, but our failure to live lives of love makes us a bit worm-like. Hymns like these have lifted up the preaching of crucifixion, and in their own way, they have lifted up the atonement of Christ for us without the sacrament of a sacrificial Communion.

There are several theories used to explain the atonement: substitution, moral, or "Christus Victor." Each has a contribution to make and a problem to overcome, and I do not see the necessity of developing the theories here. They can be analyzed, defended, or denied in the preaching of the church. And they should be. A church supper or Lord's Supper is meant to extend God's welcoming invitation to life in its fullest to believer and non-believer alike. The sacrifice of life for love is part of that invitation and is made without the stricture of the Old Testament's sacrificial system while recognizing its resonance. The reality of the cross and crucifixion point to the one lifted up from the foundation of the world (John).

The World Council of Churches, in its 1982 study, *Baptism, Eucharist and Ministry,* suggests that the Eucharist may be considered in five aspects: thanksgiving to the Father, memorial to Christ, invocation of the Spirit, Communion of the faithful, and meal of the kingdom. Why has tradition limited it only to one of these, a memorial of Christ's death? Why haven't our liturgists worked harder at helping the church celebrate the Supper in these other ways?

The answer to these two questions is fairly clear: the church has been stuck since the first century in a sacrificial and moralistic paradigm, mourning its supposed guilt instead of rejoicing in Christ's life. The church has been unable to see how Platonism placed a filter across its understanding of essence and turned it away from the Supper's focus on action. It has been locked in a belief that a re-sacrifice or a remembering of the sacrifice could make it "good," as in the old 1848 hymn by Cecil F. Alexander:

> There is a green hill far away …
> He died that we might be forgiven,
> he died to make us good.

Instead, let's consider using the seasons of the church year to cover the five themes the Council considers, reserving Lent and Advent for the times of lifting up the traditional themes of preparation for the great meal of the kingdom/*parousia*, and reserving the other seasons for celebrating the themes of thanksgiving for the created world and the infilling of the Spirit. In this way Communion could be celebrated under its many different guises, not simply in its sacrificial mode.

For a number of years, beginning in about 1975, I used the liturgies of John Gallen, SJ, for the Communion services that I celebrated because they brought wording to the prayers that did not formally employ institutional language or connote that we were to find the presence of Jesus in the elements. I had come to understand that it was perhaps as late as the ninth century that the institutional words had become required, and since I wanted to separate the Supper from its concentration on sacrifice, I found Gallen's formulations helpful. His attempt was to let liturgical prayer rise out of the lives of God's people while not allowing the prayers to become discontinuous with tradition. I changed some of the prayers in accordance with the lectionary readings (Gallen's work precedes the revised lectionary readings of 1983), and since they were written for the Woodstock Center for Religion and Worship, apparently a male institution, I made their language inclusive. And for *wine*, I used *cup*, since we did not use wine. His book, *Eucharistic Liturgies*, co-authored with Peter E. Fink and John R. Hogan, shows that the rite included institutional words. Here is an example:

Sunday of the Epiphany

Cel: Grateful for the light of Christ that today touches our lives, let us pray:

All: **Our God, we your people rise up in splendor for your light has come, your glory shines upon us. We are grateful for this light, that is Jesus Christ, brightening our lives and guiding us on the only sure path to you.**

Open our eyes that we may recognize you in all the signs you send us. Deepen our hope in this world we would make ready for your Son to come and claim it as his own.

All glory to you, Father, through your Son, Jesus Christ who draws all the world to Himself that together we may give all praise to you. Amen.

Prayer over the Gifts

Cel: Our God, from the east and from the west, from north and south, we come to sing your praises and offer You gifts. We stand tall in your presence for your glory shines upon us. You have called us your people, your own. We call you God and Father for so you have made yourself known to us.

Bless us now with the gift of your Son and grant our prayers that we may be signs to all that you are always with us. All glory be to you, God, and to your Son and to the Holy Spirit, now and forever.

All: **Amen.**

Concluding Prayer

Cel: Truly blessed are you, God our Father, for your promises are ever true to us. You are our God, a God we can trust. With the glory of your Son shining on us, may men and women come from east and west, north and south to find him living in our midst. May we who have broken bread together be signs of your peace in our world, and may we who have received your gift of love share that love with all.

We ask this in the name of Jesus Christ, your shining light, who has brightened our world with his coming, promising an even brighter day when time shall be no more. May his name be praised in our midst now and forever more.
All: **Amen**. (Gallen 160–161)

This example shows that worship may include preaching the historic testimony of Christ crucified and raised, and the Supper may also celebrate Jesus' life with a gracious invitation for others to seek redemption in Christ and find a home in a fellowship of believers that invites the outsider and the child to participate in the good news.

This is not possible if the invitation to the Supper is based on thinking that excludes rather than invites. We want all to come to that knowledge and love.

If someone teaches that the bread and cup of the Supper have an intrinsic connection to Christ's being rather than his meaning, then that person will exclude others. Tradition has pointed us in this direction, and it is from that tradition that we must turn. As Dom Gregory Dix said in *The Shape of the Liturgy*, Eucharistic worship from the outset was not based on Scripture at all, whether of the Old or New Testament, but solely on *tradition* (emphasis Dix's). I would add, "and from tradition alone we may turn."

Odyssey

In the tradition I grew up in, the preaching of the cross was
often followed with the John G. Foote 1905 hymn,

Christ our Redeemer died on the cross,
died for the sinner, paid all his due.
All who receive him need never fear
Yes, he will pass, will pass over you.

When I see the blood, I will pass over
you, When I see the blood, I will pass
    over you

Cross and Passover are mixed here, the hymn picturing the God
of the exodus passing over us like a vulture; no thought is given to
the suggestion implied that our salvation is bought with the blood
of Egypt's firstborn. It is this kind of thoughtlessness that allows
recent polls to show that torture of terrorists is highly approved of
by evangelical Christians.

I can sing these songs in my sleep, so often did I sing them as
a child, but let us turn to celebrating a Christ of life, not a God of
swooping violence.

Another gospel song, Fanny Crosby's 1868 hymn, uses better
imagery:

Pass me not, O gentle Savior, hear my
    humble cry,
While on others Thou art calling, do not
    pass me by.

Addendum

The Faith and Order Commission of the World Council of Churches imagines that we may

1. celebrate a great thanksgiving of God's goodness for everything accomplished in creation, redemption and sanctification, for everything accomplished now in the Church and in the world, in spite of the sins of human beings, for everything God will accomplish in bringing the Kingdom to fulfillment; [making] the Eucharist the benediction by which the Church expresses its thanksgiving for all Gods benefits.

2. make a great sacrifice of praise ... on behalf of the whole creation. For the world which God has reconciled is present at every Eucharist: in bread and wine, in the persons of the faithful, in the prayers they offer for themselves and for all people ... The Eucharist signifies what the world is to become: an offering and hymn of praise to the Creator, a universal Communion in the body of Christ, a kingdom of justice, love and peace in the Holy Spirit.

3. [celebrate] a memorial of the crucified and risen Christ, a living and effective sign of his sacrifice, accomplished once and for all on the cross and still operative on behalf of all humankind ... Christ himself with all he has accomplished for us, for all creation in his incarnation, servanthood, ministry, teaching, suffering, sacrifice, resurrection, ascension and sending of the Spirit is present in this [remembrance], granting us communion with himself. The Eucharist is also the foretaste of his *parousia* and of the final kingdom. (World Council of Churches 10–11)

The Eucharist is the foretaste of the parousia: look again at Exodus 24:9–11, and Luke 22:29–30.

10: WELCOMING OTHERS

In this chapter, I want to consider whether the invitation to the Supper may be broadened to invite everyone. That is not considered to be an option in traditional church life and ecclesiology, and I want to explain how thinking about the welcoming of children helped me to say yes, invite everyone, and then to talk about that "everyone."

One time I wangled an invitation to preach before another Mennonite congregation about welcoming children to the Lord's Table. The year was 1971, and I needed to do this as a prerequisite for bringing a proposal to the Triennial Conference of the General Conference Mennonite Church that children be invited to commune. Resolutions needed to reflect a wider church interest than just one person's or one church's proposal. So my pastor friend switched pulpits with me, and I chose to speak about baptism because in our tradition, only the baptized are allowed to commune. This is generally true across the church.

I wanted to show how the understanding of baptism has been used to exclude people from the table and how we might understand this differently in relation to Communion.

In the Sunday school discussion after the worship service, an interesting question was asked. "Do you welcome non-Christians to the Supper?" The logic of the question was perfectly in order: not baptized: not Christian: what about the wider implications? It had happened that at the previous Communion service in that church, a Muslim guest had been present, and I do not remember whether or not he had been invited to commune. I think not, but it had presented a problem. Not to invite seemed unwelcoming, but tradition surely seemed to suggest that he should not be.

The question triggered a memory for me. At Northwestern University, our InterVarsity chapter had once gone on a Friday evening to a Hillel Sabbath service. We were invited to enter fully into the meal, share in the wine and cakes (I do not remember everything served) and join the singing and prayers. This was all new and somewhat strange to me, not least because at that time I followed the teetotaling custom of my family and church. I had felt quite sure, however, that that Sabbath service had had some kinship with the meals Jesus had shared with his disciples. I was impressed that as outsiders we were so freely welcomed. And when I asked if we could make a contribution, the answer was, "Oh, no. We never take money in our services!" I could not help but wonder if ancient hurts over charges of money changing were still at work. But it felt good to be so welcomed.

My answer that Sunday school morning in 1971 was that I had not really thought about this, that I used the words of invitation, saying, "all who know and love Jesus" are invited to his table. This, to me especially, includes children who probably love Jesus more than adults do, and I assumed it was a generally welcoming statement.

But as I thought about it, I said I would invite a Muslim or any non-believer to participate and would need to rethink the words of invitation. Open table fellowship seems to be what Jesus was about. An outsider might honor Jesus, but not *know and love* him as tradition has shaped and intends that invitation. My reading to that point in time had not led me to understand that the words of invitation did not come into the liturgy until the ninth century. Nor had I quite come to the understanding that the meal not need be a sacrifice. Sharing bread and wine is a companionable invitation. Indeed, we share these elements with many in our own tradition who can't admit they do not truly believe or are afraid that they cannot believe enough, and the meal is not somehow ruined.

More at heart is the meaning of the Supper. What we suggest by participating in the Supper is that its action is a way to live, not that its elements have some quality that a believer is changed by eating them or an unbeliever able to sully them. Our ambivalence about the elements is a product of a long history that makes the elements holy or divine in a way our Protestant tradition does not concur with.

Well, part of our Protestant tradition. Sometimes our spirits are not where our minds are. Jesus told us to love God with all our minds, and we give homage to our minds in a long enlightenment tradition, but something within counters our belief. A long tradition among us lifts the elements almost to the category of a transubstantiated state. We may understand that the elements are not the body and blood of Jesus, that they represent an enacted parable of a way to live. We might accord them a status of conveying Jesus' presence to us, although probably not with the understanding that Lutherans bring to the meaning of the presence. Jesus is, after all, known to us in the breaking of the bread—but it is the action of breaking, not the bread itself, even though he is the bread of life.

The way we have thought this out is betrayed by our actions. We deny the elements to children and others. There have been occasions when we have not partaken of the elements lest we be "unworthy" of them. Traditions developed of taking the sacrament only once a year or, in some cases, not until one's deathbed lest some sin be the occasion for taking the sacrament unworthily and eternal salvation would be lost. And a long tradition in Mennonite and some other traditions, such as the Scottish Presbyterians, required a rigorous period of self-examination in the presence of deacons in order to partake. When I was in seminary at Second Presbyterian Church in Princeton, heir to that Scottish tradition, in the late fifties, one could present a wooden coin received the previous "Preparation" Sunday in order to show readiness to partake. Though I had not been there the previous Sunday, I was not denied Communion, a change in the rules had come.

In fairness, I must say that for Mennonites, the self-examination was intended to discover if all was right in the "brotherhood." A high concern for ethics demanded that Communion would not be taken unworthily, an appropriation of the apostle Paul's injunction to the Corinthians. How much this was divorced from a conception that the elements, once blessed, were holy is hard to say, but it is probable that that was truly the main consideration.

Children taking Communion makes some adult believers uncomfortable, visibly so. In a guilt paradigm, the complaint often is that children cannot understand the seriousness of the rite; it may be like play to them. I have never observed this, and I believe that what parents take seriously, their children will also. Furthermore, children are honored that they are welcome. Ironically, our churches like to have Seders at Maundy Thursday times, supposedly the Passover parallel to our Communion service, and a Seder very prominently features children's participation as part of the question-response liturgy and supper. Typically in these Seders, adults are more interested in the menu than liturgy or addressing the parallel being violated.

The complaint about play is actually an unhappy observation from adults who do not see that play for a child is not childishness. It lets the child work out the give and take of life at the child' own level. Is that another way of speaking of losing one's life and finding it, another way of hearing the life and death of Jesus lifted up in the invitation to the Supper? Play for a child is preparation for life, and though each play period is not analyzed in theological or life-goal terms, the lessons of play in life are not lost to us. Play can be pretty messy and uncontrolled, as is life. Books have been written about the value of looking at the "games" we play. Worship services today can also be pretty messy, but not the Communion service, please!

We Anabaptists are often charged by other traditions with neglecting children. If children are not baptized soon after birth, the argument goes, they are denied the blessing and protection of Almighty God and the certain care of the church. Worse, should they die unbaptized, they may spend eternity in limbo. I have found this the most difficult concern some Catholics face when their children become Mennonite: why can't their grandchildren be baptized?

The charge arises out of our different approach to baptism. Anabaptists disagreed with the Reformers on the practice of baptism, saying that they saw in Scripture that baptism followed the repentance of sin. This required adult comprehension. An infant cannot repent and need not, they might have added. Baptism is a symbol of commitment that invites one into membership in the church, the body of Christ. The commitment Jesus asked for required the intelligent discrimination that only an adult could exercise. The influence of Erasmus's thought with its appeal to return to the reasoning of the early church is clearly evident.

The Reformers, on the other hand, believed that the experience of New Testament believers continued the Old Testament covenants with the children of Israel. The promises were "to us and our children." Baptism replaced the rite of circumcision, an initiatory rite now broadened to welcome females as well as males. The Reformers believed that parents and godparents could take early responsibility for their children's faith, which children would later confirm with their own confession. Until such a time, children were part of the body of Christ, though not communicants.

Who was right in this disagreement over the interpretation of Scripture? Great scholars may be quoted for either side, and the answer will depend on the assumptions made about baptism and Communion. Is the sign of baptism made by parent or godparent, that is the sign of their faith, powerful in a child's life? Undoubtedly, it is. And does its power depend on the faith of the person being baptized? If a child must confirm the commitment made, does that not argue for the baptized person's willful participation? The rite of confirmation has had its proponents and detractors. The seeming parallel in the bar/bas mitzvah for the Jewish child does not quite match. That rite marks the recognition of a child as a son or daughter who has reached the age of religious duty and accepts that responsibility. A Jew who has not had the rite is still a Jew. Are we as willing to name the unbaptized, unconfirmed a Christian? Yes, we may say. God looks on the heart, not a rite. But the greater part of church history has not accepted that answer, and an unsentimental honesty may wish to concur. No rite is necessary, but declaring where you stand is.

The sublinear proof of my argument has been proved by the fact that for a good part of their history, Protestants who baptize infants have not allowed children to come to the Communion table.

The assumption about Communion is that the elements become Jesus Christ's body and blood rather than an action, a call to a way to live. This is as true for the unreflective Protestant as the committed Catholic. We may deny the idea of transubstantiation, but we bear it out in excluding children and unbelieving visitors. They must not touch the body and blood.

The Anabaptist considers the church to be a voluntary fellowship of the followers of Christ. It is not a birthright assembly, but children who are not members are part of God's realm. They belong under the aegis of heaven according to Jesus when he invited them to come to him. They do not need baptism to assure their place in the realm. The same is true of those who, according to Matthew, have looked upon the hungry and fed them, the unclothed and clothed them. They are the righteous, and their righteousness is not declared dependent upon belief or rite. As with Jeremiah (22:16), to know God is not to aver this or that, but to judge the cause of the poor and needy, to do justice. It is not a matter of mental formulations.

This testimony is unfortunately honored only in the breach today. My denomination, supposedly non-creedal, now has a multi-paged Confession to which its pastors and educators are supposed to give credence on pain of separation from their posts. Not unexpectedly, John 3:16 is given much more weight in "fellowshipping" than Jeremiah 22:16.

Church, then, could be considered something of an acquired taste. But acquiring it is a must. It is, the apostle Paul would argue, the body of Christ, and the church itself could come to declare that one cannot be a Christian without being part of the body. That the church later argued that there is no salvation outside the church ignored the words of Jeremiah and Jesus, but it meant to say that one must accept the warts and not shrug off the failures as part of one's identity as a Christian. It was an attempt to see the church as the body of Christ, both human and divine. Yes, there are hypocrites in the church, as the charge is so often leveled, and I am one of them.

The New Testament's understanding of the corporateness of belief is very different from our individualistic approach to belief. We find individual decision called for in the Bible as early as Ezekiel, who does not allow a child whose teeth are set on edge to blame his father for eating green grapes. Jesus' call to follow is issued individually. However, the spirit of our individualistic age would be quite a puzzle to the apostle Paul, who says the eye cannot say to the hand, "I do not need you."

In some ways, this is like the belief that all politics is local. The politician has to take care of the way things are at home in order to serve national interests important to the greater well-being of the constituency. When those interests—local and national—diverge, it is the trust that has been built up at home that allows skillful communication to move action forward.

So it is that the body of Christ is also local. You join a particular church, and your Christian identity must bear that particularity. There may be things you do not like in your church and do not want them defining you. But rather than walk away, you seek to bring change and to publicly avow to your church that in certain respects of church belief, you differ. You stick with it because you understand the importance of the body is the ability to act in concert. If others can tolerate your different point of view, there is no need to break fellowship.

It is not mental concurrence to a creed that makes a body. It is belonging. Children belong, and the invitation to outsiders is to come join this belonging.

This underlines the importance of the coffee hour and carry-in dinners in building bonds of friendship and care. It is not too far afield to see in these social hours the welcoming to the table that was the hallmark of Jesus' ministry. Why must the ambiance or purpose of the Communion table be any different? There are those who say that the Lord's Supper really ought to be called the church supper.

All traditions agree that baptism marks the entrance to the church. Like circumcision, it is a sign of faithfulness, and though circumcision was and is performed on the male Jew, the prophets were quite clear in repeated calls that the heart needed to be circumcised. One needed to make good on the initiatory rite. In like manner, then, the Anabaptist saw baptism as a witness that you were making good on the decision to follow Christ. They saw it as the entrance to church membership, as well.

But for all traditions—and this is the danger—linking baptism and Communion centers the understanding on the *accidental* nature of the elements; that over the centuries they have been endowed with a supernatural quality. Rather, we should understand their *intrinsic* nature—the way they call us to live.

The confusion, particularly for the Anabaptist, in making baptism the ticket for taking Communion is the suggestion that you have to be of a certain age or have a certain understanding of the sacrament or be in a state of grace to partake. Though the confessional disappeared, one was expected to confess one's sins. Again, then, the elements had holiness in themselves, which was not Jesus' original intention. This understanding developed in a short period in the first century and then was magnified out of proportion by layers and layers of tradition. The meaning of supper as an action was lost.

Return with me then to the welcoming of the other. If we think again of Jesus' ministry, we remember that he ate with all kinds of people, particularly people shunned by the religious of his day. His intention was to model how being a welcoming person modeled God's welcoming and was a foretaste of the heavenly banquet to come. He was lifting ancient tradition, recited in Abraham's stories, and reaffirming it for his day. He did not require that those he ate with agree with him. He ate with Simon the Pharisee, who did not show him courtesy, and Judas, who betrayed him. He ate with "sinners," but eating was not an endorsement of their activities. It was an invitation to accept a different approach to life. That invitation was not bound by his, or his community's, definition of sin. It was an invitation to accept God's welcoming grace.

The church, Jesus' body, should do no less. Instead, words common to the rite are "fencing the table" and "close communion." The latter term is quite an oxymoron. It is actually "closed" and "close" only to its beleaguered communicants, shut off from the world Jesus came to. Is it earnestly possible to "commune" with others when the parameters are set as to what must be believed? Can

I hear another's truth if only my opinion is valid? Close communion is the opposite of Jesus' call to the feast, lifting up Isaiah's, "Ho, everyone who thirsts, come to the waters; and you that have no money, come, buy and eat! Come, buy wine and milk without money and without price." (55.1)

At a time when the world needs welcoming love, a time of division and divisiveness between faiths and nations and political and sociological viewpoints, there is no reason for the church to model the world's approach. It hurts that my denomination has so misunderstood the openness of Jesus that it has closed the Lord's Table to persons of other faiths. What a failure to see that the open table is both an invitation and a way to model amid all of the violence that there is another way to live. It is evangelism in the best and truest sense. In this critical period of Christian-Muslim relations, we need our rituals to reach out to all our neighbors rather than close them out.

But, incomprehensibly, my denomination also closes its doors to believers of homosexual orientation, or makes them live closeted lives, denies blessings their unions, and threatens its ministers with expulsion if they transgress the "Confession" in blessing those unions. Like the church of the first century, it is easier to turn to the Levitical laws than to lift up and live by the freedom Jesus came to bring, preposterously missing our selectivity in selecting which of those laws we will follow. My church would not deny Communion to a homosexual person or a supporter of abortion rights, but its heavy repetition that we welcome those who truly repent of their sins makes it clear that the elements are not for everyone. Eating the bread and drinking the cup brings us a share in the eternal life of Christ, not a witness to his way of life.

With these actions, the church has come to the apex of misunderstanding of our Lord and has conformed itself to the world that eats only with those who can return the favor or those who are of the same kosher faith. Hear Jesus to the contrary! It's sad to say that few in the church understand or are willing to discuss these things as part of their Table fellowship. But then it is no longer a dialogical table fellowship, but a rite.

What is more antithetical to Jesus' welcoming message than using the Lord's Table to exclude "sinners," homosexuals, and politicians who do not toe the church's line? We could ask for some kind of consistency in toeing the line on capital punishment, "just war," and abortion, but the true problem is that Jesus does not exclude those who differ on any of these. He welcomes friend and denier alike. The Table is meant to be a place of meeting, not a creedal bar.

There is a beautiful story in the New Testament that bears out what I have been saying in this chapter. It is the story of the apostle Paul's shipwreck. On his way to Rome, where he would later die, the ship with 276 persons aboard ran afoul of bad weather and for fourteen days languished in danger of going down; for fourteen days the storm was so bad that no one had been able to take any food. Then, as the fifteenth day was about to dawn, Paul urged his shipmates to take food and in what has been called the four-action shape of the Eucharist, Paul took bread, gave thanks, broke the bread, and ate. Those on board took heart, threw the cargo overboard, took food, and were saved. The context was the ultimacy of salvation, both for Paul and his unbelieving shipmates, just as it is the context for us every time we come to the Communion table. Sermons have rung the changes on what it means to throw the cargo overboard.

Now, the argument has been that since this was before a shipload of unbelievers, it could in no way be a Eucharist rite but was simply an example of a Jew observing a grace before a meal. Isn't it interesting that the scholars who make this assessment claim a four-action shape of the Eucharist when Jesus feeds the multitude? How many believers were there? They were probably all Jews and thus of Jesus' own "church." But they did not understand what he was about. They wanted to make him a political king!

The parameters of the actions taken by Paul and Jesus are the same: a very real salvation is at stake—for Jesus, Paul, and the mariners. For Paul and the mariners the story is action; Eucharistic action, and as dogma, the Eucharist interpretation can be rejected.

In another great story, we have no liturgical action, but we have a meal of welcome that conveyed forgiveness: the story of the Prodigal Son's return. Who of us is not prodigal? Who is not the elder brother? Who of us does not long for the welcome that acceptance gives?

Every celebration of the Lord's Supper is an invitation to believe for all who are there. Every celebration of the Lord's Supper is an invitation to throw the cargo overboard that is threatening shipwreck to our lives. Every celebration of the Lord's Supper is a welcoming sign of the heavenly banquet where all are invited and all are offered salvation.

Let us welcome the other!

Odyssey

Thomas Edward Frank, of the Candler School of Theology, recently lamented that the distinctiveness of ordination is being lost. He asks, perhaps arguing with the Wesleys,

> if United Methodism still constitutes a church—[that is, by his definition, an institution that values a priestly role]—or whether it has become a lay movement. This question has nothing to do with the abilities, integrity or faithfulness of local pastors [who are not seminary trained], nor the witness and mission of the local church they serve. Many non-ordained pastors do a terrific job and are much loved by their people. But our practices make no sense ecclesiologically. What do we think we are doing? Increasingly, we are saying that ordination does not matter. (Frank, *Christian Century,* July 13, 2010)

My argument in these pages is that we priest one another, a first century concept. Let us ordain each other. Ecclesiology was born in later centuries.

11: "COME AND SEE"

The next day John was standing there with two of his disciples, when he saw Jesus walking by. "There is the Lamb of God!" he said. Hearing this, the two disciples went with Jesus. Jesus turned and saw them following him and asked, "What are you looking for?" They answered, "Where do you live, Rabbi?" ... "Come and see," he answered.

—John 1:35–39

My goal has been to show how our understanding of the Lord's Supper developed and how that development has made the Supper become a time of heavy repentance, or a means to make us good, and has led to the exclusion of children and outsiders. The journey has taken us across the years and between the lines of Scripture and through speculation, where only hints could suggest why things developed as they did.

I hope that something of the warm invitation we find in Jesus' words, above, has come through. He was inviting and not excluding. That should be the welcome we project as his followers in our central liturgical act. Where and how we live is the focus.

My goal has also been to show that the liturgists' apparent decision that the developments in the Mass from the third or fourth through the twelfth centuries were to be accepted as the foundation of liturgical worship rites need not be the final word. To grant that the final word ignores the possibility that the meals Jesus celebrated with his disciples and friends were simply meals (but not *simple* meals, as metaphors are not simple). The last meal according to the earliest gospel understandings can still simply be that for us, and it can be so in a liturgical way.

We have seen how Jesus' meals were welcoming meals, meals with outsiders, sinners, deserters, disciples, and believers. We want to see now how we can continue that today.

As I have reminded here, a sacrament grows out of these simple roots. The tree's developments are caused by what happened in church life in the first century and the later divide between the agape meal and the Eucharist in the second century, probably lacking the institutional words, and then, finally, the influence of neo-Platonism in the third and fourth centuries.

Nowhere is there a scriptural mandate for the words of invitation, which by tradition have become penitential ("You who truly and earnestly repent of your sins …") or even subtly exclusionary ("All who love and know the Lord Jesus"), as in my tradition, fencing the table. The Episcopal and Reformed traditions use the beautiful *sursum corda* ("Lift up your hearts" … We lift them to the Lord") and sentences of welcome ("Come unto me, all you who labor …"), but the sentences are directed to the household of faith.

There is a time for confession of sin. It should come early in worship, indicating our hesitancy to approach. Upon absolution, the service proceeds to the issues of living the new creation and thanksgiving for God's care and goodness. My contention is that confession need not be part of the Supper, but if it is, that confession can be appropriate for all humankind. As those welcomed explore the invitation, the long history of salvation's goal of bringing us to the kingdom may be explored.

Lord's Supper or last supper? I vote for the latter. The difficulty is that even in my tradition, which has weakly tried to follow a Lord's Supper tradition within Sunday morning worship, the Communion service is an addendum. Without an agape meal later in the day,

Holy Communion is celebrated as a Lord's Supper with themes of repentance and forgiveness of sin.

First, the very denial of the elements to children and outsiders suggests that the elements are something more than bread and wine. If it is argued that there is "something more" that may be missed or misused by the outsider, one must answer: of course, there is something more, and that is what we are inviting children and outsiders to experience. It is not the substance of bread and wine we are celebrating but what they point to, as the Didache claimed: grapes and wheat gathered from the hillsides are symbols of life and nurture, the life Jesus lived and invites us to.. The something more is this: we celebrate his action, not his being.

Are we the guardians of "the host," or could the Host just possibly not be undone when nibbled upon if we are going to grant that sacramental view? Jesus fed an unbelieving crowd who desperately wanted to believe. He invited the crowd to take up the cross with him; he did not prescribe a "bread of immortality" for them.

When I commune, I give thanks for the symbols of sustenance from the foundations of the world and for the world's sustenance, but I pray more that my life may be marked by a gift of brokenness and by being poured out.

Second, when we do not invite unbelievers and Muslims and persons of other faiths, the issue is not their possible sinfulness. Who of us is not sinful? The problem is ours. We are making the supper something it is not and was not intended to be: a meal these persons must not touch rather than a meal that says this is the way we think it best to live. "Come and see!"

And third, how may we escape the sirens who beckon us to use the supper in moralizing ways, to make us good, to build our characters? Surely, their call is the way to shipwreck. The supper is about acting as Jesus acted. Sitting with prostitutes, blessing tax collectors, telling soldiers to turn the other cheek. If acting as Jesus acted builds character, well and good. The trouble is that it is hard to separate a Boy Scout mentality (doing a daily good deed) from what is being intended by character building, or singing of Jesus' dying to make us good. Jesus was not dying to make us good. It would be better to follow the Alcoholics Anonymous model: I am a sinner, and I need help, but I am not thereby excluded. Alas, if you are a sinner, tradition says you are *not* supposed to come, and thereby you have a catch-22.

In no way am I denying or minimizing sin. We are sinful. But let's make our repentance in our prayers, not at the supper.

Yes, we recognize that worship, as John Howard Yoder says, "contributes to ethics something foundational of love or hope—what ordinary usage might call motivation" (33). Yoder argues that because of this sharing, bread can become a paradigm for soup kitchens and hospitality houses. Thus Communion shapes our character to behave ethically but does not thereby make us "good." Goodness belongs to God, and we are the sinners God invites to the table. Let the outsider name any separation from God. The supper is not meant to give us forgiveness because we eat it but to be a means of testimony to God's welcoming inclusion.

Still, should something be said programmatically?

The Catholic and Orthodox traditions conceive the worship service to be centered on the celebration of Communion. Preparation is made through confession, Scripture, prayers, and the homily. Orthodox theology is oriented toward the glory of the coming life rather than sacrifice, but the celebration's closeting makes the elements more important than the action. It was not intended in Orthodoxy, according to Alexander Schmemann, that the iconostasis should bring this separation to pass. But, he says, that is what has happened. Priests in both traditions are made more important than laity. They are endowed with a different power.

The Reformed tradition initially kept the Eucharist/supper separate by requiring attendance at a service of preparation on stated days. The separation of preaching and supper in the Reformed tradition grew from a need for instruction. The supper was not the only means to being forgiven for a sin. Worship offered that.

The Eucharist says, *This is the way I want you to live; take the bread of life.* Have those who campaign for weekly Sunday morning Communion not understood forgiveness apart from the supper? They insist that Luther and Calvin never wanted to give up the weekly celebration, but their logic suggests that mediation of forgiveness through the sacrament should lead to daily observance.

There need not be a problem in integrating worship and Communion service, preaching enriching the supper theme of the day or season. Seeker-friendly worship should prepare outsiders for Communion that is inviting rather than one that demands repentance they are not yet ready for.

Experience has not proved this to be easy to do, and the general assumption of some good Catholics, for instance, appears to be that the truly important part of the service is the Communion. For some, to miss the first part of the service is not crucial.

Trial balloons have not revealed much support for the weekly observance of Communion in Protestant circles. One church that I know of did so for a quarter of Sundays, with a Sunday school class meeting afterward to process the approach Sunday by Sunday. After a quarter, the church resumed its celebrations on festival Sundays.

It seems to me that we have three choices. First, to keep the present approach: making the supper a time of forgiveness and finding salvation. Second, integrating the supper into our morning worship as a call to follow Jesus into new life, a welcoming to those outside the faith. Third, separating worship and supper as the first century church did.

I would suggest that the third choice should be the programmatic goal we seek today. The course taken by the early church remains viable: let worship be worship, and let holy meals be meals. This is so even though the distinction between the last supper and the Lord's Supper may not be understood. Instinctively or intuitively, Protestants seem to have turned from the steady diet of sacrifice found in the Lord's Supper tradition. Whether this would change if one could successfully re-focus the meal to an inviting marriage supper of the Lamb, the heavenly banquet, is hard to say.

I realize that not pursuing weekly Communion is a block to discussion with a greater part of the church. That is unfortunate, because the issue of essence or action may thereby be dropped. Such a decision greatly affects the discussion of church unity and the recognition of others' understandings. It may subvert reflection that every Sunday's Mass is about action, not essence or transubstantiation of the bread and cup. Reflection on essence centers on personal rightness with God; reflection on action centers on doing God's work in the world. My grandchildren remind me that the word *Mass* comes from the Latin word *missa*—be dismissed, depart to serve—which focuses on action.

Generations of worshiping Christians have felt the purpose of Sunday worship is getting right with God, when it should be praising God for God's work in the world of which they can be a part.

I hope that by considering these issues, my own tradition may be strengthened. Our present approach of either adding the supper or integrating it into the worship service is not working well. It confuses what a meal and worship are really meant to be about. Worship is directed to God. It requires confession and absolution. A meal is about welcoming another, celebrating the other's presence.

Some of our churches have thought the solution to lie in having people come forward to tables for Communion at the end of the worship service. Unfortunately, this generally results in an interminable service, not one where fellowship happens or where people can be forthcoming.

The Church of the Brethren has sought a return to the agape supper of the first century, the evening meal of the book of the Acts, and the meal of the young church into the second century. Its character as a resurrection celebration has not been recovered in the few services I have attended. The washed foot was more readily understood as the washing away of sin than the call to walk with Christ.

In the Church of the Brethren and other Brethren associations of the Anabaptist movement, a light meal is held with brief prayers and singing, perhaps a short meditation, and then Communion, followed by foot washing. I have only attended such an agape three times, making it risky for me to comment. But since these occasions were intended as an introduction to the practice, I can say that what I observed was more about confession of sin than a welcoming banquet. Basins and towels were brought to the tables where we had eaten. We did not separate by sex, although women washed the feet of women and men the feet of men. (It is interesting to note how modern sensibilities form ritual.)

The foot washing itself was in each instance directed toward confession of sins or testimony to one's present experience with Jesus. The Brethren movement's origination in Pietism was clearly present, and any evaluation of the movement must view it through the Pietistic screen.

Perhaps if foot washing had come at the beginning, I might have felt welcomed. But as it comes at the end or in the middle of the meal in John—Jesus becomes aware that something fundamental to their meeting has not occurred—it seems fated to force us to be self-revealing rather than feel welcome. I did not experience it as welcoming. That may have been due to my nervousness over participating in something new. I am not very good at sharing where I'm at spiritually with a stranger. Surely, foot washing was meant to be welcoming. Why must we verbalize something that was intended as an enacted parable? Verbalization is a result of Pietism, not John 13. The interchange between Jesus and Peter does not have to invite confession of sin or introspection and discussion of where one is in spiritual pilgrimage. It was a simple act by which Peter could show that he was wholly in touch with Jesus' mission, the soles of his feet signifying body, mind, and spirit in his willingness to follow.

Given this gospel history, I would like to pursue adapting the agape service for worshipers today. Given the long history of the supper and its popular understanding for salvation, the change I suggest will be seen as radical. But with a New Testament "last supper" focus on the resurrection, this could be the vehicle we need for our own more regular observation of "as often as you do it." I doubt that we can combine worship with the Lord's Supper weekly on Sunday mornings and achieve a last supper practice as Jesus envisioned for the meals. That takes the agape, the inviting of neighbors and friends for the pure reason of wanting to invite them, to tell them about what you have found exciting in life and, when it seems appropriate, to say how Jesus the Lamb of God fits in your life, but not to do so in worship format. This would help the supper focus on sharing rather than sacrifice, hopefully on listening and accepting.

We are acquainted with using meals for other purposes: signing on to college development drives, getting life insurance, entertaining ways to protect our investments, or a sales talk to consider buying a piece of lakefront property. We know these invitations. This is not that. There should not be a sub-rosa reason for gathering. What the agape is meant to do is to provide an occasion to invite your friends just because you want to enjoy the fullness of life together. German Mennonites call it the *faspa* (a kind of supper vesper), a Sunday late afternoon meal you invite your friends to, a low-key way to share your life in Christ. Whether one could integrate that into morning worship is doubtful. It did not happen in the first and second centuries.

Here is my suggestion: We have a perfect carrier in the Sunday morning coffee hour. Adapt the agape to our coffee hour fellowship times, a feature of many church services today. Let it, without formality, have a genuine welcoming act, a handshake instead of foot washing. Handing a small hot towel to visitor or friend for quick rejuvenation or bussing one another on the cheek in place of a formal kiss of peace would be welcoming.

Let the fellowship times be graced with a sense that what we do here is a foretaste of our welcome in heaven. Don't make it a formality nor feel that there must be verbalization.. As with the feeding of the thousands, signal a deeper meaning with action: lift your eyes to heaven, give thanks, and break the bread (or candied almonds? Once in Nazareth, Israel, in the fellowship time after worship in a Latin Rite church where we were invited to take the sacrament, we had candied almonds; another time at Nablus in an Anglican church we had marvelous petit fours in the fellowship time). There does not need to be talk about what we are doing; we should trust our actions to carry the message.

In my pastorates, I have argued that the fellowship hour is one of the most important things we do. It is here we catch up on what is happening in our lives—not deeply, but with a depth of caring that can lead to that. It is here we make newcomers welcome. It is here we communicate the acceptance we have found in Jesus Christ.

Eucharist is thanksgiving. In a day of abounding negativity, greed, corruption, terrorism, and despair, we need to be called to thanksgiving for our wonderful world, the care of family and friends, the places where justice triumphs, the institutions that bring order, the gifts we have been given, all saying yes to life, thanks to God, Eucharist. (Don't say all this in one prayer!) But doing this, we do not exclude repentance or our need for forgiveness; raising such thanks reminds us of where we are coming from. We are not dualists— us good, them bad. We know our complicity in evil, but calling ourselves to thanksgiving allows us to name God's graciousness to us and our dependence upon God.

As chaotic as most of our coffee times are (some persons taking the opportunity to get a piece of church business done, others eager to talk with a friend, everybody maneuvering to too few coffee stations), I know this would all take some doing!

We could be more intentional about the time's purpose, asking attendees to pause for a moment, but go with the chaos! As long as this agape is not far off in difficult-to-find fellowship halls, the coffee–Kool-Aid time is almost a perfect setting for welcoming children and others. Take a leaf from cocktail parties: a crowded space with an accomplished host or hostess can work welcoming wonders. Have someone move around to engage statuettes and wallflowers!

Perhaps there could be the sounding of a bell (shades of the Mass!) and a brief word of greeting and invitation to a prayer of thanksgiving. It does not have to be remarked, but as one who has on numerous occasions had to clear his throat at a crowded meeting in a fellowship hall in order to get attention, I would welcome the tinkling of a bell.

Unfortunately, our coffee times are mostly communion in one kind—only coffee or juice. The agape approach would need coffee cake or nut bread for breaking. It would take some advance planning but would not be prohibitively expensive.

If we would work intentionally at making the coffee hour an agape time, not overly burdening it with religious rubrics but allowing it to provide koinonia fellowship, it could come close to the first century model of a two-service approach, worship and agape. Celebrating the presence of Christ—that is, that the church is the body of Christ—need not be heavy with rite or rubric. Welcoming others as he did is the proof of his presence. Let conversations and friendships build on that welcome. A few seconds of heralding this as a time together for a purpose of the celebration of life need not defeat the coffee hour.

And if we continue as we are, what about Communion? If we make it part of the worship service, at the very minimum it should not be an add-on but integral to the service, incorporating the service's themes. However many times we celebrate the supper, let it celebrate the resurrection (yes, we do not get to resurrection without the passion). Celebrating the resurrection may make us consider a weekly observance, since every Lord's Day is said to be a small Easter.

What does the Communion service mean to us? If it is a sacramental experience of ingesting the body and blood of Jesus, his essence, it is also a call to living as he lived. How does the morning Communion service reflect that call?

Invite everyone. Say, "Once there was a ruler who prepared a wedding feast for his son; he sent his servant to tell the invited guests to come to the feast …!" Or, "Hurry, Zacchaeus, I must stay at your house today!" Or, tell the story of the two disciples walking to Emmaus after the resurrection who invited Jesus to stay with them, and he did: "He sat down to eat with them, took bread, said the blessing, broke the bread, and gave it to them, and then their eyes were opened ..." Note that Jesus asks to stay or is asked to stay and how this always ends up with him sharing a meal. Some scholars think *stay* is a way of saying *eat*. Each vignette here is open to quick embroidery. Only a sentence is needed. Remind us on occasion, "This man sits with sinners and eats with them." With us!

Let the prayers pick up the themes of the day's gospel or response to the sermon. In liturgical churches, the prayers of confession and thanksgiving in the Lord's Supper are set prayers of some length. They are beautiful, and to many people, they define the proper approach to God. But let the Spirit lead and keep your prayers broad enough to include the world God so loved and the church that is Christ's body; keep them personal enough to bear out the promise that God cares for each one of us.

"Where do you live, rabbi?" "Come and see."

Odyssey

The Church of Christ (Disciples) celebrates Communion each Sunday. I attended a morning worship service in the church in Wadsworth, Ohio, in the seventies and was interested to find the elders rather than the pastor leading the Communion service. Perhaps in the Reformed tradition, the elders are ordained; still, I felt the practice pointed to an openness to not having to have ministerial ordination. That only the ordained may preside brings us back to the second century, when bishops replaced the laity in the blessing, and makes the focus center on the elements rather than the action.

Recently I contacted the Reverend Martha Everhard of that Wadsworth Church to ask how she invites people to the table. She replied that she says, "All who confess their faith in our Lord Jesus Christ are invited to take the bread and cup." Their hymnal, she said, uses these words: "This is the Lord's Table and Christ invites you to share this meal of grace. Christ recognizes you and looks on you with favor. Christ befriends you and wants you within his circle. Count yourself among Christ's disciples by partaking in this feast of fellowship."

The hymnal's words are inclusive. I appreciate them, though counting oneself among Christ's disciples may foreclose an outsider's feeling of welcome.

The odyssey has not ended. Let the dialogue continue.

AFTERWORD

The theology of the Lord's Supper is grandly summarized in Paul's letter to the Ephesians: "Now in Christ Jesus you who were once far off have been brought near by his blood. For he is our peace, in his flesh he has made both Gentile and Jew into one and has broken down the dividing wall, that is, the hostility between us" (2:13–14). This is the witness of the table as family and neighbor sit together. Breaking bread symbolizes Jesus with us as at Emmaus. Ancient table fellowship celebrates the peace we long for. "Indeed, when he came he proclaimed the good news: 'Peace to you who are far and peace to those near.' Through him and in one single Spirit the two of us have access to the Father" (2:17–18).

God is greater than all our systems, and at the table we acknowledge that, enjoying the access to God we grant each other. Underneath this, not mentioned but recognized, we understand that sacrifice and death have purchased that peace; they maintain our peace.

Paul's says Gentile and Jew. We may say unbeliever and believer, Arab and Jew, male and female, and gay and straight. At the table, we all partake of a deeper unity and share a humanity that asks for bread.

This is our faith: as we exhibit the grace of Christ's presence, as we trust the other in breaking bread together, as we have been accepted and so we accept, as peace is made and enmities dissolved, we join the heavenly banquet.

Welcome to the banquet!

Glossary

Apocalyptic Affording a revelation, often considered a result of some traumatic event or vision and thus biblically pertaining to the book of Daniel, Revelation, or Mark 13; of late, the understanding is that Jesus' birth and ministry must be understood as apocalyptic.

Chaburah The fellowship meals Jesus shared with disciples that form the pattern for his last meal.

Didache Anonymous second century treatise also known as *The Teaching of the Twelve Apostles.*

Ecclesia The gathering of Christ's disciples; the called, translated church in the Acts; from this term, *ecclesiology* refers to understandings governing church life.

Eschaton Eternity; *eschatology* is the understanding of final things.

Eucharist Thanksgiving; Communion.

Excursus A detailed discussion of a point raised in the book.

Gnostic   Pertaining to knowledge understood by one's own thinking or gained secretly by revelation.

Parousia   The Second Coming or Advent of Christ's return to earth or heaven. Church Father Irenaeus said that the Parousia is not a place in the future; rather it means to arrive at wisdom only in Christ.

BIBLIOGRAPHY

Baillie, D. M. *The Theology of the Sacraments.* New York: Charles Scribner's Sons, 1957.

Barth, Markus. Rediscovering the Lord's Supper. Atlanta: Westminster John Knox, 1983.

Bausch, William J. *A New Look at the Sacraments.* Notre Dame, IN: Fides/Claretian, 1977.

Beker, J. Christiaan. *Paul the Apostle.* Philadelphia: Fortress, 1980.

Borg, M. J and N. T. Wright. *The Meaning of Jesus: Two Visions.* San Francisco: HarperSanFrancisco, 1998.

Brown, Raymond E. *The Gospel According to John.* The Anchor Bible, vols. 29 and 29A. Garden City, NY: Doubleday, 1970.

———. *The Birth of the Messiah.* Garden City, NY: Doubleday, 1977.

Brown, Sally A. *Cross Talk.* Louisville: Westminster John Knox, 2008.

Cahill, Thomas. *The Gifts of the Jews.* Anchor/Doubleday, 1998.

Chilton, Bruce. *A Feast of Meanings.* Leiden: E. J. Brill, 1994.

———. *Jesus' Prayer and Jesus' Eucharist.* Valley Forge, PA: Trinity International, 1997.

———. *Rabbi Jesus. New York:* Doubleday, 2000.

——— and Jacob Neusner, ed. *The Brother of Jesus: James the Just and His Mission.* Louisville: Westminster John Knox, 2001.

Cochrane, Arthur C. *Eating and Drinking with Jesus: An Ethical and Biblical Inquiry.* Philadelphia: Westminster, 1974.

Collins, John J. *The Bible After Babel: Historical Criticism in a Postmodern Age.* Grand Rapids: Eerdmans, 2005.

Cousar, Charles B. *A Theology of the Cross.* Minneapolis: Augsburg Fortress, 1990.

Crossan, John Dominic. *Jesus: A Revolutionary Biography.* San Francisco: HarperCollins, 1994.

———. *The Birth of Christianity: Discovering What Happened in the Years Immediately After the Execution of Jesus.* San Francisco: HarperOne, 1998.

Cullman, Oscar. *Early Christian Worship.* London: SCM, 1950.

Dix, Gregory. *The Shape of the Liturgy.* New York: Seabury, 1982.

Driver, Tom F. *The Magic of Ritual.* San Francisco: HarperSanFrancisco, 1991.

Dylan, Bob. "I Dreamed I Saw St. Augustine." *John Wesley Harding.* Recorded October 1967. Columbia Records B000OTNUWW. Vinyl. Originally released in 1968.

Eller, Vernard. *In Place of Sacraments*. Grand Rapids: Eerdmans, 1972.

Erickson, Craig Douglas. *Participating in Worship: History, Theory, and Practice*. Louisville, KY: Westminster John Knox, 1989.

Finger, Reta Halteman. *Of Widows and Meals*. Grand Rapids: Eerdmans, 2007.

Fiorenza, Elizabeth Schussler. *In Memory of Her*. Crossroad, NY, 1983.

Freiday, Dean. *Speaking as a Friend*. Newberg, OR: Barclay, 1995.

Friedmann, Robert. *The Theology of Anabaptism*. Scottdale, PA: Herald, 1973.

Gallen, John, Peter E. Fink, and John R. Hogan. *Eucharistic Liturgies: Studies in American Pastoral Liturgy*. Paramus, NJ: Newman, 1969.

Gonzalez, Justo L. ed. *Westminster Dictionary of Theologians*, Louisville: Westminster John Knox, 2006.

Greeley, Andrew M. "Empirical Liturgy: The Search for Grace." *America*. Vol. 157, No. 15 (November 21, 1987): 379–383, 390.

————. *The Great Mysteries: Experiencing Catholic Faith from the Inside Out*. San Francisco: Harper & Row, 1976.

Heim, S. Mark. *Saved from Sacrifice: A Theology of the Cross*. Grand Rapids: Eerdmans, 2006.

Helwig, Monica K. *The Eucharist and the Hunger of the World*. Kansas City, MO: Sheed & Ward, 1992.

Hunsinger, George. *The Eucharist and Ecumenism: Let Us Keep the Feast*. Cambridge UP, 2008.

Jeremias, Joachim. *The Eucharistic Words of Jesus*. Philadelphia: Fortress, 1966.

Jones, Cheslyn, Geoffrey Wainwright, and Edward Yarnold. *The Study of the Liturgy*. New York: Oxford UP, 1978.

Keifert, Patrick R. *Welcoming the Stranger*. Minneapolis: Fortress, 1992.

Klaassen, Walter. *Anabaptism: Neither Catholic nor Protestant*. Waterloo: Conrad, 1973.

Koenig, John. *The Feast of the World's Redemption*. Harrisburg, PA: Trinity International, 2000.

Kreider, Eleanor. *Communion Shapes Character*. Scottdale, PA: Herald, 1977.

Lang, Bertrand. *Sacred Games: A History of Christian Worship*. New Haven: Yale, 1997.

Lazareth, William H. *Growing Together in Baptism, Eucharist and Ministry: A Study Guide*. Geneva: World Council of Churches, 1982.

Levenson, Jon D. *The Death and Resurrection of the Beloved Son*. New Haven: Yale, 1993.

———. *Resurrection and the Restoration of Israel*. New Haven: Yale, 2006.

———. *Sinai and Zion: An Entry into the Jewish Bible*. New York: HarperCollins, 1985.

Lietzmann, Hans. *Mass and Lord's Supper: A Study in the History of the Liturgy*. Leiden: E. J. Brill, 1979.

The Liturgy of the Lord's Supper: The Celebration of Holy Eucharist and Ministration of Holy Communion. Prayer Book Studies XVII. New York: Church Pension Fund, 1967.

Macy, Gary. *The Banquet's Wisdom*. New York: Paulist, 1992.

Martin, Ralph P. *Worship in the Early Church*. Grand Rapids: Eerdmans, 1964.

Marty, Martin E. *The Lord's Supper*. Minneapolis: Fortress, 1980.

Marxsen, Willi. *The Beginnings of Christology*. Philadelphia: Fortress, 1969.

———. *The Lord's Supper as a Christological Problem*. Philadelphia: Fortress, 1970.

Meeks, Wayne A. *The First Urban Christians*. New Haven: Yale, 1983.

Milavec, Aaron. *The Didache*. Collegeville MN: Liturgical Press, 2003.

Neufeld, Thomas R. *Recovering Jesus: The Witness of the New Testament*. Grand Rapids, MI: Brazos Press, 2007.

Nolan, Albert. *Jesus Before Christianity*. New York: Orbis, 1988.

Pelikan, Jaroslav. *The Christian Tradition: A History of the Development of Doctrine*. Vol. 1. Chicago: University of Chicago Press, 1971. 100–600.

———. *Jesus through the Centuries: His Place in the History of Culture*. New York: Harper& Row, 1986.

Perry, John Michael. *Exploring the Evolution of the Lord's Supper in the New Testament.* Kansas City, MO: Sheed & Ward, 1994.

Powell, W. R. Chilton. *Prayer Book Studies XVII: The Liturgy of the Lord's Supper: The Celebration of Holy Eucharist and Ministration of Holy Communion.* New York: Church Pension Fund, 1966.

Rempel, John D. *The Lord's Supper in Anabaptism.* Scottdale, PA: Herald Press, 1993.

Richard, Lucien. *What Are They Saying about the Theology of Suffering?* New York: Paulist, 1992.

Sanders, E. P. *The Historical Figure of Jesus.* London: Penguin, 1993.

Schmemann, Alexander. *The Eucharist: Sacrament of the Kingdom.* Crestwood, NY: St. Vladimir's Seminary, 1988.

Schmidt, Dan. *Taken by Communion.* Grand Rapids, MI: Baker, 2003.

Schwager, Raymund. *Jesus in the Drama of Salvation: Toward a Biblical Doctrine of Redemption.* New York: Herder & Herder, 1999.

Schweitzer, Albert. *The Quest of the Historical Jesus.* New York: MacMillan, 1956. 403.

Sloyan, Gerhard S. *Why Jesus Died.* Minneapolis: Fortress, 2004.

Smith, Gordon T. *A Holy Meal.* Grand Rapids, MI: Baker, 2005.

Soulen, R. Kendall. *The God of Israel and Christian Theology.* Minneapolis: Fortress Press, 1996.

Stark, Rodney. *The Rise of Christianity*. San Francisco: HarperCollins, 1997.

Thurian, Max. *Ecumenical Perspectives on Baptism, Eucharist and Ministry*. Geneva, World Council of Churches, 1983.

Torvend, Samuel. *Daily Bread, Holy Meal: Opening the Gifts of Holy Communion*. Minneapolis: Augsburg Fortress, 2004.

Wainwright, Geoffrey. *Doxology: The Praise of God in Worship, Doctrine, and Life: A Systematic Theology*. New York: Oxford UP, 1980.

————. *Eucharist and Eschatology*. New York, Oxford UP, 1981.

Weaver, J. Denny. *The Nonviolent Atonement*. Grand Rapids, MI: Eeerdmans, 2001.

Webster, Jane S. *Ingesting Jesus: Eating and Drinking in the Gospel of John*. Atlanta: Society of Biblical Literature, 2003.

Welker, Michael. *What Happens in Holy Communion?* Grand Rapids: Eerdmans, 2000.

Willimon, William. *Sunday Dinner*. Nashville: Upper Room Books, 1981.

Witherington III, Ben. *The Christology of Jesus*. Minneapolis: Fortress, 1990.

————. *Making a Meal of It: Rethinking the Theology of the Lord's Supper*. Waco, TX: Baylor UP, 2007.

World Council of Churches. *Baptism, Eucharist and Ministry (Faith and Order Paper No. 111, the "Lima Text")*. 1982.

Wright, N. T. *The Meal Jesus Gave Us: Understanding Holy Communion*. Louisville, KY: Westminster John Knox, 2002.

Yoder, John H. "Sacrament as a Social Process: Christ the Transformer of Culture." *Theology Today* 48.1 (1991): 33–44.